NEW APPROACHES IN SOCIOLOGY
STUDIES IN SOCIAL INEQUALITY, SOCIAL CHANGE, AND SOCIAL JUSTICE

Edited By

Nancy A. Naples
University of Connecticut

A ROUTLEDGE SERIES

NEW APPROACHES IN SOCIOLOGY
STUDIES IN SOCIAL INEQUALITY, SOCIAL CHANGE, AND SOCIAL JUSTICE
NANCY A. NAPLES, *General Editor*

CONTEXTUALIZING HOMELESSNESS
Critical Theory, Homelessness, and Federal Policy Addressing the Homeless

Ken Kyle

Routledge
New York & London

Published in 2005 by
Routledge
Taylor & Francis Group
270 Madison Avenue
New York, NY 10016

Published in Great Britain by
Routledge
Taylor & Francis Group
2 Park Square
Milton Park, Abingdon
Oxon OX14 4RN

Printed in the United States of America on acid-free paper
10 9 8 7 6 5 4 3 2 1

International Standard Book Number-10: 0-415-97442-9 (Hardcover)
International Standard Book Number-13: 978-0-415-97442-4 (Hardcover)
Library of Congress Card Number XX-XXXXX

Library of Congress Cataloging-In-Publication Data

Kyle, Ken.
    Contextualizing homelessness : critical theory, homelessness, and
    federal policy addressing the homeless / Ken Kyle.
        p. cm. -- (New approaches in sociology)
    Includes bibliographical references and index.
    ISBN 0-415-97442-9 (hardcover)
    1. Homelessness--United States. 2. Critical theory. 3. Homelessness--
    Government policy--United States. I. Title. II. Series.

HV4505.K95 2005
305.5'692--dc22   2005008753

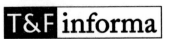

Taylor & Francis Group
is the Academic Division of T&F Informa plc.

Visit the Taylor & Francis Web site at
http://www.taylorandfrancis.com

and the Routledge Web site at
http://www.routledge-ny.com

For my mother and father,
who've always kept a home for me

&

For Peptol

Contents

Acknowledgments

First and foremost, I would like to thank Anne L. Schneider who guided me through this research from the very start. Not only did she offer encouragement and research support throughout my doctoral studies and dissertation research, but she also offered the occasional push and poke when one was needed. I am in your debt, thank you. I am also grateful for the assistance of Peg Bortner, David Theo Goldberg, and Pat Lauderdale who offered their expertise and support throughout my doctoral studies. Many thanks. Along the way, a number of friends and colleagues offered editorial suggestions and comments on various chapter drafts. Thank you to Tara McBride, Susan Jones, Judy Stein, and Tania Israel. My thanks also to Barbara Duffield of the National Coalition for the Homeless and George Ferguson of the Department of Housing and Urban Development. Both made me feel at home during my repeated visits to their respective offices and both provided valuable aid in locating resource materials and references. Also, I am particularly indebted to George Ferguson who granted me an impromptu interview when I first showed up at his office. In addition, I received technical support from Mary Fran Draisker at ASU, and Ilhan Kucukaydin and Kathy Ritter at PSU. Many thanks to each of you. Also, Penn State Capital College's School of Behavioral Sciences and Education and its Graduate Research Support office each contributed funds for copy-editing. It is certainly appreciated. I could not have completed this project without the support and friendship of Holly Angelique, Diana Weaver, Robert Brem and Ed Taylor. Muchas gracias my friends!

Foreword

Critical theory always has to come to terms with a seemingly inherent contradiction between the language and ideas it uses to confront contemporary injustices, on the one hand, and its long-term goal of an applied analysis that will enable oppressed people to recognize and understand their own oppression, its causes, and avenues of resistance that they might take. Ken Kyle, in this very fine critical analysis of homelessness, acknowledges that the work comes much closer to the first goal than to the second. But in setting out almost a classic model of how to go about a critical analysis that contributes to understanding homelessness and to the evolution of post modern critical theory, he makes a genuine contribution to each.

In the first chapters of the book he provides a clear, concise, and coherent account of the evolution of critical theory, its modern and post-modern strands, and the criteria he uses in his critical account of homelessness. Chapter 2 contains an account of the methodology, which is a form of contextual constructionism, particularly as it concerns public discourse and public policy identification of the social construction of homeless people. As a form of rhetorical analysis, he turns to the idea of ideographs–an "ordinary language term" found in political discourse, narratives, and characterizations that underpin narratives.

In chapter 3 he begins the serious analysis of homeless policy when he focuses on the Stewart B. McKinney Homeless Act of 1987. Kyle traces the origins of the act, the ways the statute divides the homeless population into a number of different "types" and how it characterizes the homeless in terms of mentally ill, families with children, persons with drug or alcohol problems–largely avoiding the long-term historical view of homeless as single white men who are portrayed as beggars, tramps, bums, and so forth. This chapter describes how homeless people were portrayed, in popular culture, the press, by the President (who is reported to have said that many of them are "homeless by choice"), in Congressional discourse, by the social scientists who were busy trying to count them, and in the statute itself. He finds three general views of homelessness. Conservatives tended to believe that the homeless were individually responsible for their own fate and that government had no responsibility for them. Liberals tended to view the homeless as victims of broader social and economic forces, and that the federal government should provide assistance. Reformers or "educators" were in favor of federal aid to the homeless, but viewed them as misguided and personally responsible for their own fate. Later, in discussing the alms houses, he added a fourth category, in which the homeless were viewed as "virtuous Christians"—the meek who are to inherit the earth–and who should be looked after by the church.

The fourth chapter traces the emergence of homeless public policy from the English vagrancy laws in the 13th century through the New Deal–setting the context for the McKenney act. In the pre-vagrancy law period, it was customary for the church to care for the poor, but a law of 1274 actually forbade churches from helping the homeless, on the grounds that the churches hardly had enough resources to care for themselves. Within a decade, another law forbade anyone from helping those who were idle or vagabonds. The first vagrancy laws in the 14th century criminalized the giving of alms to any unemployed person of sound mind and body, and criminalized idleness itself. Many years later, some acts began to focus on problems of unemployment, but nowhere did the monarchy assume there was a public responsibility to help care for the poor. On the other hand, Churches were ordered, by statute, to help care for the poor who were unable to work. These periods are characterized as moving from the Virtuous Christian period—which had to be restrained by law in order to avoid a proliferation of beggars and exacerbating the labor shortages–to a regime Kyle calls the "keeper of orders" in which work is required of everyone who is able. The coming of the Alms houses in the U.S. represents the emergence of the reformers who believed that homeless were misguided and needed to be reformed, but also believed that the government was responsible for helping care for them and bringing about their reformation. As Kyle traces the history of homelessness in conjunction with the history of poverty, it becomes clear that all of the regimes developed categories of the poor, some of whom were poor even though they worked; others who could not work but because of age or infirmity deserved to be cared for, and (the undeserving) who preferred idleness and had not self respect. The New Deal ushered in the fourth theme—a liberal theme in which it was acknowledged that social and economic conditions of the great depression had produced a group of people who, through no fault of their own, were homeless and poverty-stricken. Furthermore, the federal government took upon itself responsibility for the welfare of the people, thus ushering in the welfare state system in the U.S. Kyle points out that this system perhaps was never fully accepted, even though it was not seriously challenged until the 1996 welfare reform act.

In chapter 5, Kyle turns to the role of science in homelessness and presents a fascinating account of how science has been viewed throughout the centuries; how much of the "cutting edge" of the science of previous centuries today is nothing but myth; and how social science came to two quite distinct views of homelessness that could be used by proponents as well as opponents of federal assistance. Kyle recognizes the double-edged sword of science as it can offer potentially useful guidance but at the same time if embraced uncritically can foster undemocratic values.

One of the advantages of taking such a long historical perspective is, as Kyle points out in the conclusion, that the liberal period of time when poverty and homelessness were recognized as one of the chronic conditions of capitalism's booms and busts and government programs to provide assistance, may itself have been the aberration. Even though it was a 50 or so year aberration, a liberal approach to poverty and homelessness has never been the norm and it may never have been fully accepted in the United States.

Anne Larason Schneider
School of Justice and Social Inquiry,
Arizona State University

Chapter One
Critical Theory and Homelessness

"Short Thigh"

Hear we are sharing this

moment of hear we are. Wanting

to tell you I got love on my

mind so don't try to take it from

me. Can't you see we have all

the time in the world

> Hear we are
>
> Hear we are

Brite beautiful day

Brite beautiful night

(Peptol, 1997)

Peptol, the author of this poem is a homeless man I met in Tempe, Arizona, on a cool, damp, drizzly December afternoon. Even though I met him, I do not know his full name. In fact, I no longer know whether or not he is still without a home. He approached me as I was having a cup of coffee and reading a book on critical theory outside a local coffee shop. Peptol explained that he wrote poems and sold copies of his work for a dollar a piece to raise money to pay for his overnight shelter and food. He said that he disapproved of panhandling. He explained that he wanted to earn his money.

This was not our first encounter. He had approached me a few times during the past year and each time, I purchased a photocopy of his latest poem. I bought a copy of this poem and set it aside. It was only after he left and I finished reading the chapter I was working on that I read his poem. Unfortunately, I did not run into him at any of our usual haunts during the eight months or so following that encounter before I moved away. Since that last encounter, I have not had the opportunity to ask him to comment on my interpretation of his work or to even ask him his full name.

Peptol's poem and our encounter serve as an excellent introduction to the methodological concerns and approaches guiding this work. The poem can be read at a number of levels. It can be read first and foremost as a plea for us to hear and acknowledge him and others experiencing similar conditions. This call seems clear enough given the experiences of many homeless people. Some homeless individuals explain that they are treated as if they are invisible. Many people literally and figuratively avert their eyes from the homeless. Many people refuse to make eye contact with homeless people or pretend they do not see them at all. Similarly, researchers and census-takers warn that many homeless people remain out of view despite attempts to find them. In a way, despite our best efforts to enumerate (accurately determine the number of) the homeless, some do indeed seem to be invisible.

At another level, Peptol asks us to recognize him and other impoverished people, not as a people whose existence is based upon their status of having no homes, but rather as one of us, as one of the "we" engaged in reading and interpreting this poem. Read this way, it is a plea for us to see each other for our commonalties. We are all "sharing this moment" of hearing or acknowledging "we are." Put another way, Peptol calls for us to see ourselves, the homeless and those of us with homes—the non-homeless, the "homed," if you will—alike as joined together in this historical moment. Peptol's "we" are all engaged in interpreting and making sense of this moment and in attempting to make ourselves heard. Or perhaps better, "we" are all engaged in constructing ourselves against the backdrop of historical time. In this way, "we are sharing this moment of hear we are."

With this reading in mind, Peptol's labor/poem can be read as a signpost pointing the way we must critically engage the social ills of homelessness, poverty and oppression in general. Moreover, as a signpost, the poem offers directions on how we may begin to address these ills meaningfully. I suggest that Peptol's repeated emphasis on being aware of our position, "Hear we are," parallels our need to situate ourselves historically—homeless and "homed," unemployed poor and working poor, underclass, lower class, middle class and upper class alike—in relation to one another, in relation to socio-economic practices and institutions, and in relation to earlier historical epochs. Attempting to address homelessness and explain how the ongoing retrenchment in social welfare policies is possible requires an intense, multi-layered, or "thick" contextualization of homelessness.

Furthermore, Peptol's act of writing and selling his work draws attention to the power of societal norms and expectations to affect our values and our self-perceptions. Accordingly, his actions point to the need of the oppressed to actively participate in their own emancipation and to the need for advocates and academicians to facilitate these emancipatory struggles. Similarly, my awkward interaction with Peptol is telling. It highlights the ironic and difficult relationship between the researcher, theorist or critical analyst who works at an abstract level, seemingly aloof, and the oppressed person who experiences overt domination in her or his daily life.

CRITICAL THEORY

The critical engagement implicitly called for through my reading of Peptol's work is not novel. Such an approach has been developed by critical theorists, and it is within the tradition of critical theory that I situate my work. However, there are numerous understandings of critical theory. Therefore, a few words concerning the various meanings of the term, the dominant strands of critical theory, and my own understanding of critical theory are in order.

I employ a very broad definition of the term "critical theory." I ground this understanding of critical theory in the practice of critique. At their most basic level, critical theories are those theories that involve critique. But critique itself has many meanings and many conflicting interpretations. Furthermore, as a practice, critique has its origins in antiquity. However, I limit my use of the term critique to those practices derived from or consistent with Karl Marx's methodological approach.[1]

In his work, *Grundrisse,* Marx lays out what he considers to be an appropriate methodological approach for the study of society. To illustrate this approach, Marx offers nineteenth century political economists' use of the abstract concept, population, as a counter example or foil. He writes:

> It seems to be correct to begin with the real and the concrete, with the real precondition, thus to begin, in economics, with e.g. the population, which is the foundation and the subject of the entire social act of production. However, on closer examination this proves false. The population is an abstraction if I leave out, for example, the classes of which it is composed. These classes in turn are an empty phrase if I am not familiar with the elements on which they rest. E.g. wage labour, capital, etc. These latter in turn presuppose exchange, division of labour, prices, etc. . . . Thus, if I were to begin with the population, this

would be a chaotic conception [*Vorstellung*] of the whole, and I would then, by means of further determination, move analytically towards ever more simple concepts [*Begriff*], from the imagined concrete towards ever thinner abstractions until I had arrived at the simplest determinations. From there the journey would have to be retraced until I had finally arrived at the population again, but this time not as the chaotic conception of a whole, but as a rich totality of many determinations and relations. . . . The concrete is concrete because it is the concentration of many determinations, hence unity of the diverse. It appears in the process of thinking, therefore, as a process of concentration, as a result, not as a point of departure, even though it is the point of departure in reality and hence also the point of departure for observation [*Anschauung*] and conception. (Marx, 1973, pp. 100–101)

Understood in this way, a critical theory approach minimally involves unpacking taken-for-granted social relations and institutions. Yet Marx's call to break down abstractions logically should not stop at this point. Underlying Marx's approach is what appears to be a correspondence view of language; i.e., a view that words or symbols (signs) ultimately refer to concrete things (signifiers) in at least some instances. However, this view is contested by many (e.g., Derrida, 1974; Baudrillard. 1983a). Unfortunately, Marx was either not privy to or did not take account of developments in the field of linguistics sufficiently (Saussure, 1989), and he clearly did not have access to later developments in the field of semiotics (e.g., see Silverman, 1983; Echo, 1992). For example, in a series of lectures delivered between 1907 and 1911, Ferdinand de Saussure argued that the systems of signs and symbols that make up language are ultimately arbitrary. He explained:

> Some people regard language, when reduced to its elements, as a naming process only—a list of words, each corresponding to the thing that it names. . . . This conception is open to criticism at several points. It assumes that ready-made ideas exist before words; it does not tell us whether a name is vocal or psychological in nature . . . finally, it lets us assume that the linking of a name and a thing is a very simple operation—an assumption that is anything but true. (Saussure, 1989, p. 3)

Simply put, the relationship between any particular sign and the idea or concept it calls to mind is based solely on social convention. Therefore, returning to Marx's aforementioned quote, there is no "simplest conception" that can be reached.

Still, Marx was aware that a term such as population does not refer to a ready-made idea. He saw population as a complex, "chaotic conception of the whole" made up of simpler ideas; hence the need to undertake the type of critical analysis he promotes. However, Marx appears to have accepted the idea that at some level some words do actually signify some ideas—"the simplest conception." From Saussure's perspective, not only are "classes but an empty word" but all words are ultimately empty of intrinsic meanings. (I discuss the process of meaning-assignment through language in greater detail in chapter 2.) Had Marx incorporated this perspective into his work, he probably would have altered his argument slightly. He might have argued that through painstaking analysis, a holistic concept such as population can be shown to be grounded upon many other apparently less complex conceptions such as classes, which are themselves based upon other apparently less complex conceptions such as labor, and so on and so on, *ad infinitum*. Accordingly, he could have argued that "the concrete [appears to be] . . . the concrete, because it is a combination of many objects with different destinations, i.e., a unity of diverse elements. . . . it therefore is a process of synthesis, as a result, not as a starting point."[2]

Therefore, I argue that a methodological approach driven by Marx's logic would also entail unpacking taken-for-granted terms, concepts and language itself, as well as social relations and institutions. In essence, a critical theory approach involves making the apparently concrete appear contingent at numerous levels, but it involves doing so in a way that allows the critical theorists to actively engage in changing the world. Therefore, at this most basic level, many seemingly diverse methodological perspectives fall under the rubric, critical theory. For example, the genealogical studies of Michel Foucault (1978; 1979), the structural analyses of Quentin Skinner (1988) and Roland Barthes (1972a; 1980), and the feminist analyses of Maria Mies (1986) and Claudia von Werlhof (1988) are all critical theory pieces. But these divergent strands of critical theory share other features.

Again drawing from—or at least consistent with—Marx's work, I hold that critical theories are interested in seeing an end to or a reduction of oppression. In this way, critical theory aspires to be an emancipatory practice; i.e., an activity that eliminates or reduces the constraints and suffering people experience due to cultural, political, social and/or economic arrangements, practices and institutions. Critical theory strives to achieve this goal by providing in-depth analyses of such arrangements, practices and institutions. Kai Nielsen writes: "Critical theory sees itself as an intellectual tool or intellectual device in the long process of achieving *enlightenment* and *emancipation*. These are the essential aims of critical theory without which there would be no critical theory" (1992, p. 269).

This emancipatory mission is founded upon critical theory's presumption that humans are enmeshed in cultural and linguistic traditions, economic and political systems, religious beliefs, social mores, taboos and social values that limit our freedom and, to some extent, delimit the possible. Many critical theorists view these as components of ideology.[3] For those critical theorists who are comfortable with the notion, ideology is seen to play a crucial role in perpetuating social ills such as homelessness, poverty, bigotry, and oppression in general. From this perspective, when individuals unconscientiously accept aspects of their society's ideology as proper, legitimate or natural, they act as agents of that ideology. In doing so they perpetuate the social relations prescribed by that ideology, including social relations that may be detrimental to the individuals enacting them. Individuals acting in this way are said to experience false consciousness. For example, in the 1980s President Reagan enjoyed great popularity among blue-collar workers and even among many union members. Apparently swept up in the rhetoric of responsibility, free trade and competitiveness, many of these workers and union members supported the Reagan administration's initiatives to defund many social programs, break the power of trade unions, and freeze the minimum wage. Yet each of these administration efforts negatively affected the living conditions of union members and blue-collar workers. As another example, the GOP and George W. Bush enjoyed wide-spread support among U.S. military personnel and veterans during the 2004 campaign and election; this despite their substantial reduction of support in Veterans' benefits and services (Bush & GOP screw veterans but good!, 2003), and their policies that put many active duty, national guard, and reservists in harm's way via their involvement in foreign wars in Afghanistan and Iraq.

According to Raymond Guess: "The very heart of the critical theory of society is its criticism of ideology. Their ideology is what prevents the agents in society from correctly perceiving their true situation and real interests; if they are to free themselves from social repression, the agents must rid themselves of ideological illusion" (1981, pp. 2–3). Similarly, Stephen Leonard writes: "Domination is characteristically underwritten by theoretical self-understandings . . . that are systemically grounded in ontological theses that are neither defensible nor coherent" (1990, p. 262). Critical theorists respond to this ideological illusion and/or domination by conducting ideology critique. Drawing from Guess' work, *The Idea of a Critical Theory* (1981), Nielsen suggests that when ideological critique is done well, it

> can 'break . . . the *compulsion to believe* in the legitimacy of the repressive social institutions.' . . . Reflection 'alone can't do away with real

social oppression but it can free the agents from unconscious *complicity* in thwarting their own legitimate desires.' . . Moreover, it may be the case that 'delegitimization of oppression may be a necessary precondition of the political action which could bring real liberation.' (Nielsen, 1992, p. 282).

Accordingly, critical theorists assume that emancipation requires that individuals participate in their own liberation through self-reflection. Guess writes that the purpose of self-reflection is "to bring the agents to realize that the coercion from which they suffer is self-imposed, thereby dissolving the 'power' or 'objectivity' of that coercion and bringing them to a state of greater freedom and knowledge of their true interests" (Guess, 1981, p. 70; see also Friere, 1970; cf. Foucault in Ebert, 1994, p. 24). As Richard Box explains, "critical theory aims to create conditions in which a fully conscious public enacts change" itself (1995, p. 5).

However, some postmodern critical theorists object to the very notion of ideology. Instead of ideology, they prefer to use the concept discourse; i.e., utterances as they emerge in verbal, written and visual texts or as they are made manifest through various cultural practices.[4] For example, Foucault argues that the notion of ideology has three inherent problems.

The first is that, like it or not, it always stands in virtual opposition to something else which is supposed to count as truth. Now I believe that the problem does not consist in . . . seeing historically how effects of truth are produced within discourses which in themselves are neither true nor false. The second drawback is that the concept of ideology refers, I think necessarily, to something of the order of a subject. Third, ideology stands in a secondary position relative to something which functions as its infrastructure, as its material, economic determinant, etc. For these three reasons, I think this is a notion that cannot be used without circumspection. (Foucault, 1984a, p. 61)

In other words, because ideology is associated with notions of false consciousness, it presupposes an underlying truth. For postmodern critical theorists, freedom as it is widely understood, emancipation, and "the truth" are not possible. In addition, because individuals or classes are purported to experience false consciousness through the workings of ideology, the concept ideology carries within it or at least fosters the idea that individuals or classes (subjects) exist independent of and/or prior to the workings of ideology. Postmodern critical theorists strongly disagree with this position. As Friedrich Nietzsche explains:

> Just as popular superstition divorces the lightening from its brilliance, viewing the latter as an activity whose subject is the lightening, so does popular morality divorce strength from its manifestations, as though there were behind the strong a neutral agent, free to manifest its strength or contain it. But no such agent exist; there is no 'being' behind the doing, acting, becoming; the 'doer' has simply been added to the deed by the imagination—the doing is everything. (1956, pp. 178–9)

In fact, Foucault went as far as to (in)famously describe subjects as "effects" of discourses (1979, p. 28). Finally, crude Marxist notions of ideology hold that ideology is driven by economic forces and relations of production and that ideology serves to perpetuate the status quo. Postmodern critical theorists argue that this is a far too simplistic and overly determined understanding of social reality. While they may acknowledge that economic relations play a role in facilitating social reality, they do not accept that they play the greatest role. Furthermore, they point out that there are multiple competing, and even resistant, discourses in circulation at all times.

Postmodern critical theorists value awareness of the workings of discourses, practices and social institutions, although such views may appear to lead to apathy, despair and nihilism.[5] Jane Caplan contends, "It is possible . . . to concede that subjectivity, beliefs, knowledge, claims of truth are contingent on the different ways in which a subject is positioned, and to explore (and debate) the conventions of their production as knowledge, truth, etc., without falling into the abyss of nihilism . . ." (1989, p. 271). Indeed, Foucault argues:

> 'The ethico-political choice we have to make everyday is to determine which is the main danger. . . . My point is not that everything is bad, but that everything is dangerous. . . . If everything is dangerous, then we always have something to do. So my position leads not to apathy but to a hyper-and pessimistic activism.' (reprinted in Simons, 1995, p. 87)

Postmodern critical theorists perform critical analyses of discourses and social structures in order to make us better aware of how we participate in fostering our own *un*freedom. But in doing so, postmodern critical theorists take pains to avoid making reference to a transcendental subject, i.e., an individual, collective group, class or even species that exists outside of or prior to history and/or language. Similarly, they work to avoid presenting current social relations as the *necessary* result of earlier events or movements. As Nietzsche explains:

the whole history of a thing, an organ, a custom, becomes a continuous *chain* of reinterpretations and rearrangements, which need not be causally connected among themselves, which simply follow one another. The 'evolution' of a thing . . . is a sequence of more or less . . . independent processes of appropriation, including the resistances used in each instance, the attempted transformations for purposes of defense or reaction, as well as the results of successful counterattacks. (1956, p. 210)

Accordingly, postmodern critical theorists are suspicious of traditional historical analyses (Bennett, 1987; cf. Hume, 1992).

Nevertheless, something akin to ideologies can be studied by postmodern critical theorists. They conduct deconstructive readings of discourses and offer genealogical accounts of regimes of truth. In relation to Foucault's methodological approach, Benjamin Sax explains: "Although individual discourses often compete with and even contradict one another, they, nevertheless, form themselves into historically identifiable 'regimes of truth'" (1990, p. 130). Sax further explains that the discourses underpinning particular regimes of truth are not overly complex. "'It isn't so much a matter of analyzing discourses into its unsaid, implicit meaning,' Foucault claims, 'because . . . discourses are transparent, they need no interpretation, no one to assign them a meaning'" (Sax, 1990, p. 130). Accordingly, some postmodern critical theorists can engage regimes of truth from a genealogical perspective. As Foucault explains, this entails "a form of history which can account for the constitution of knowledge, discourses, domains of objects, etc., without having to make reference to a subject which is either transcendental in relation to the field of events or runs in its empty sameness throughout the course of history" (Foucault, 1984a, p. 59). Therefore, postmodern critical theorists illustrate the contingency of discourses—and by extension, the contingency of social relations founded upon these discourses—by pointing out the rhetorical moves through which discourses and regimes of truth are constructed and maintained (cf. Caplan, 1989, p. 267). From Foucault's perspective, it is not possible to free ourselves from the grips of power; nevertheless, resistance is possible. Accordingly, for Foucault, the awareness that comes from engaging in these deconstructive practices allows us the choice to resist consciously those structures we find most repugnant.

For analytical purposes, Stephen Leonard divides critical theory into two strands: modern critical theory as represented by Jürgen Habermas and his supporters, and postmodern critical theory as represented by Foucault. However, both modern and postmodern critical theories share a number of concerns. As examples, both strands are suspicious of instrumental rationality's ascension over other forms of reason (e.g., see Horkheimer, 1947; Forester, 1993; cf. Foucault, 1965; Schram, 1995b). Both are leery of our society's zealous acceptance of, and faith in, modern technology (e.g., see Marcuse, 1964; Adorno & Horkheimer, 1972; Kyle, 2000). And both strands are critical of the power that the media and mass culture wield in contemporary society (e.g., see Adorno, 1990).

Still, despite these commonalties, the two strands differ in three important ways. As discussed earlier, they disagree over the question of ideology's usefulness. They also disagree on the merit of the Enlightenment project and its underlying assumptions. Similarly, they differ greatly over the question of whether or not critical theory's emancipatory goals can be grounded upon universally valid principles.

The Enlightenment designates a Western philosophical movement arising in the late seventeenth and early eighteenth centuries. As Immanuel Kant explained, "Enlightenment is man's [sic] exit from his self-incurred tutelage. Tutelage is man's inability to make use of his understanding without direction from another" (1963, p. 3). Thus, proponents of the Enlightenment believed that human reason would overcome the ignorance and superstition of earlier times. Insight into, and ultimately control over, the laws of nature and humankind would be gained through the employment of rational methods such as scientific inquiry. Generally speaking, the Enlightenment is characterized by skepticism toward pre-Enlightenment dogmas and values, belief in the inevitability of human progress, reliance upon empirical approaches to science, and faith in the independence of the individual. Accordingly, the Enlightenment is founded upon the assumption that there is one objective truth. It assumes that there are invariable laws governing the universe, including human behavior and social relations. Also, it assumes that these laws and the truth are knowable. Finally, it assumes that individuals are autonomous, rational agents who exist prior to and independent of social structures.

On one hand, postmodern critical theorists are highly suspicious of what they term "meta-narratives." Meta-narratives are widely circulating stories about who we are as a people. These stories sustain and legitimate particular activities, relations, commitments and social institutions. As evidenced by observing contemporary U.S. society, various meta-narratives co-exist, sometimes supporting one another, sometimes competing with one another. For example, Judeo-Christianity, anthropocentricity, and patriarchy are three mutually reinforcing meta-narratives that underpin Western civilization. Accordingly, postmodern critical theorists view the

Enlightenment as presented above as another meta-narrative (Norris, 1982; Hassan, 1987).

In contrast to the relatively seamless development of human relations and society depicted in meta-narratives, postmodern critical theorists argue that human relations and social reality are much more disjointed and fragmented (Lyotard, 1984). Furthermore, Foucault (1984b, p. 38) differentiates between the Enlightenment understood as an event and humanism; i.e., the meta-narrative made up of the recurring themes and assumptions attributed above to the Enlightenment. As Jon Simons reports: "Humanism is, for Foucault, a series of doctrines which tie us to our subjectivities and to particular notions of personhood. These ties prevent us from attaining maturity and bind us to the authority of the forces that limit us" (1995, p. 17). From this perspective, set notions of persons independent and/or free of discourses are antithetical to the attitude of the Enlightenment as described by Kant above. Postmodern critical theorists would point out that set notions of personhood prevent humans from making use of their understanding. In essence, such set notions function as "direction from another" (Foucault, 1984b). Therefore, it can be argued that Marxism is consistent with many aspects of the Enlightenment project. And in fact, many postmodern critical theorists level the same criticisms against Marxism that they do against Enlightenment political projects and Enlightenment philosophy (e.g., see Foucault, 1981; Derrida, 1994).

One the other hand, modern critical theorists argue that the Enlightenment project still has emancipatory potential. However, this potential is not tied solely to natural laws or the truth as it is uncovered through the careful application of instrumental reason to the study of empirical reality. While modern critical theorists employ instrumental rationality in their critical analyses, they do not see it as the only useful form of rationality. Modern critical theorists place great faith in communicative rationality's potential to facilitate the development of valid normative principles (Habermas 1984; 1987a), and thus, to serve as the basis for just social relations and just decision-making (Dryzek, 1990; Kyle, 2004).[6] As Thomas Mautner explains, Habermas and his supporters argue "that there is an orientation towards understanding and consensus inherent in communicative action, an orientation which can serve as a basis for the diagnosis and remedy of particular social pathologies" (Mautner, 1996, p. 175). These inherent qualities serve as the basis for communicative rationality.[7]

Ideally, modern critical theorists turn to communicative rationality for guidance in determining normative standards and values. These values serve as a standard against which contemporary social arrangements are judged. Furthermore, modern critical theorists argue that critical theory *must* have a valid normative foundation as a necessary safeguard against the chaos of unchecked relativism. They argue that critical theory cannot be justified without such principles (Habermas, 1987b). Because of this, "Habermas has consistently sought . . . a normative foundation for social critique in the dimension of human communication" (Mautner, 1996, p. 175). Therefore, these communication-derived principles necessarily serve as the basis for formulating emancipatory practices and for conducting critique.

However, postmodern critical theorists voice serious doubts concerning the existence of any inherent qualities in communication. They emphasize the oppressive potential of the modern critical theorists' aspirations to see the enlightenment project through to its conclusion. In particular, theorists such as Julia Kristeva (1993) and Richard Rorty (1989) argue that there are serious political ramifications associated with aspirations for the truth or for universal principles. Indeed, postmodern critical theorists view such desires as dangerous, and they point to Fascism, Nazism, and Stalinism to support their claims. Although Habermas no longer argues that even the ideal speech situation promises one correct standpoint on which to base critical theory (see Mautner, 1996, p. 175), postmodern critical theorists suggest that even discussion of an ideal speech situation implicitly supports the view that one correct universal standpoint is possible—hence their strong and persistent opposition to modernist critical theory. Because of these concerns, postmodern critical theorists do not offer universal principles to guide behavior. Instead, they offer only context-specific critiques of discourses, systems, social relations and institutions that constrain us and make us *un*free.

Despite these differences, both strands are similar in that their theorizing typically remains at a very abstract level. Leonard writes: "Both models of critical theory share a common frame of reference in the assumption that political choices must be grounded in universally applicable normative claims, or, failing this, that all normative claims rest on ultimately arbitrary preferences" (1990, p. xviii). He suggests that because of this shared assumption, protagonists from both camps have become ensnared in sterile debate with one another over epistemological matters. He chides participants from both sides for losing sight of "what critical theory should be about" (Leonard, 1990, p. 6): namely, the forwarding of emancipatory politics and/or theory. He writes:

> Critical theory . . . has usually meant showing that the notion of
> understanding the world as it really is is a philosophically incoherent,

theoretically deficient, and politically pernicious ideal. The social disciplines . . . must play a role in changing the world—and changing it in ways that can help 'emancipate' those on the margins . . . by providing them with insights and intellectual tools they can use to empower themselves. (Leonard, 1990, p. xiii)

By focusing upon the meta-theoretical issues described above, such critical theorists do critical theory a disservice. Or put another way, the vast majority of work by critical theorists falls far short of its potential.

Leonard presents three crucial requirements that a critical theory must satisfy if it is to remain true to its purposes:

> First, a critical theory must provide a coherent account of how present circumstances and the systemic self-(mis)understandings of social agents are in large part responsible for the unfreedom many of them suffer. Second, critical theory must provide an alternative vision of social relations that those who are oppressed can embrace as their own. But these two theoretical moments can be realized only if a critical theory embodies a philosophical self-understanding that can underwrite a translation of its theoretical claims into an idiom that is intelligible to the communities of sufferers to whom it is directed. (1990, p. 4)

I incorporate each of these criteria into my understanding of critical theory. However, I suggest that a fourth requirement is implicit in these three. I hold that a critical theory must be self-reflective; that is, it must be critical of itself and its role in fostering "systemic self-(mis)understandings" (see Nielsen, 1992, pp. 266–7). Considered one at a time, these four criteria act as important guidelines for this work.

The first requirement of a critical theory necessarily entails a thick contextualization of the matter at hand cutting across a number of levels. A thorough critical theory of homelessness would require an interrogation of the material, social, political and cultural conditions experienced by the poor, homeless and oppressed, as well as those experienced by the affluent and those with homes. It would require consideration of the structural factors that facilitate these conditions. More explicitly, a comprehensive critical theory of homelessness would require a methodical, in-depth examination of the economic, class, gender, racial, ethnic and sexual relations, etc., that characterize the particular moment and society in which homelessness is experienced. It would require critical review of the laws and public policies designed to alleviate and/or affect these problems. It would also require an interrogation of the discourses and rationalities underlying and facilitating these relations. Furthermore, it might also require an interrogation of these very concepts themselves.

With these criteria in mind, I work to further the development of a critical theory of homelessness in the United States. In the next four chapters, I focus primarily on the role that language and rhetoric play in supporting homelessness. In particular, I examine the way that language, social constructions within public policy, and notions of homelessness, work and science facilitated homelessness in the U.S. toward the end of the twentieth century.

I do so for three related reasons. First, I contend that language and rhetoric play so fundamental a role in shaping and perpetuating the status quo that we cannot address the economic underpinnings of homelessness and poverty successfully unless we first understand the workings of language and rhetoric. Therefore, conducting a critical analysis of rhetoric's building blocks and of its workings should add a valuable component to the overall explanation of homelessness. In doing so, hopefully it will aid efforts to ameliorate the suffering experienced by those without homes, support the efforts of the homeless to work toward their own emancipation, and perhaps, ultimately, facilitate the eradication of homelessness fostered by contemporary economic, social and political institutions and arrangements in the U.S.

I am not alone this hope. For example, Sanford Schram argues that "interrogating discourses provides a way to challenge structures of power that constrain what is politically possible" (1995a, p. XXIV). Similarly, Michael Katz argues that "the vocabulary of poverty impoverishes political imagination" (1989, p. 3). I suggest that this "vocabulary of poverty" not only circumscribes the political arena, but it also conveys societal expectations to those experiencing poverty.

For example, Anne L. Schneider and Helen Ingram (1994; 1997) argue that the portrayals of the people set to receive benefits or burdens by a policy (i.e., target populations) within public policies, and the way in which policies are structured and implemented affect members of those target populations. Thus, if a policy design presents welfare aid recipients as passive agents dependent upon public assistance, then aid recipients may indeed come to behave that way. Similarly, Handler and Hasenfeld (1991) argue that social policies mold our understandings of the "deserving" and "undeserving" poor through the symbols and practices they employ. Therefore, critical examination of the way that rhetorical portrayals and social constructions of the homeless affect the self-perceptions of homeless persons and the views of non-homeless persons is a necessary step toward empowering the homeless.

But the "vocabulary of poverty" is not limited to policy designs or certain words used in political debate. It permeates society in numerous rhetorical texts. It is reproduced in everyday conversations through the employment of certain evocative words, or ideographs: terms that call forth certain images and/or expectations even as they seem to foreclose conscientious consideration of those images and/or expectations. It emerges in the narratives we subscribe to and tell others: for example, a person's belief that a self-help or twelve-step program turned her life around. It is embodied in national myths such as manifest destiny and America as a land of unlimited opportunity. It is passed along through visual and literary images, and it is bolstered by national symbols and icons. Accordingly, in my analysis I examine a great variety of rhetorical texts. These texts range from scientific texts to laws to political speeches to poetry. While some of these texts may have had greater circulation at a particular time or in a particular arena, all play a part in perpetuating the "vocabulary of poverty."

Second, critical theory is traditionally considered to be synonymous with the modernist critical theory of Marx, the Frankfurt School, and Habermas. Because of this, postmodern methodological approaches are not employed as often as they might be in applied critical theory works and in applied social constructionists work. Accordingly, I offer this effort as an example of an applied critical theory piece that draws from both the modern and postmodern strands of critical theory. Therefore, I draw upon approaches often associated with postmodern critical theory in my analysis.

Third, as discussed above, much of critical theory tends to remain at an abstract level even when it explicitly aspires to be contextually aware (e.g., see Young, 1990a; Kyle, 2004). I argue that the authors of some case studies grounded in social constructionist theories fail to historically situate their analyses adequately (e.g., see Donovan, 1993; Hogan, 1995). Similarly, the same may be said for some academic work on homelessness as well. I suggest that these and other applied works would benefit from a more in-depth examination of the widely circulating stereotypes, discourses, ideographs and literary images that underlie the particular problem they are addressing. Critical consideration of these factors should provide insight into how those experiencing oppression may recognize and work to overcome their own internalized stereotypes. Furthermore, it should also assist the oppressed in developing strategies for opposing negative social constructions and stereotypes that are arrayed against them (cf. Best, 1995, p.349).

The second requirement of a critical theory entails consideration of how social relations might be arranged so that the "systemic self-(mis)understandings" that facilitate *un*freedom may be prevented. I address this requirement in chapter 6, Conclusions & Critical Review. However, as discussed above, the desire for universal guidelines to reduce or eliminate oppression has been a stumbling block for critical theorists. Leonard offers an insightful way to move beyond this apparent impasse (1990, p. 7). He explains that the arguments leading up to this impasse are actually misguided. He argues that critical theory does not need to provide universal principles in order to be emancipatory. There is nothing inconsistent or wrong with a critical theory providing a case-by-case analysis of social problems. In fact, he suggests that this is actually in keeping with the spirit of Marx's own notion of critical theory as emancipatory praxis. As discussed earlier, Marx's method of critique demands a thick contextualization of social reality. But why should this contextualization not be extended to social theorizing and to the development of critical theory itself (cf. Derrida, 1994)? Accordingly, critical theory must be seen as contingent, partial and case-specific. And it is upon this understanding of an applied critical theory that my work is based.

In keeping with critical theory's fourth requirement, I specifically conduct a critical review of this work in the concluding chapter. Furthermore, I have undertaken this project with the third and fourth criteria in mind. I hope that this is apparent in my writing style, choice of vocabulary and examples.

PROJECT PLAN

Given my desire to help enable homeless persons to improve their situations and to reduce the oppression they experience, I strive to meet the four criteria outlined above. Accordingly, I present explanations of a number of terms and methodological perspectives used throughout the work in chapter 2 so that my work may be more accessible to readers.

As suggested earlier, the way we present and talk about the homeless facilitates their continued oppression. Knowledge of those biases that influence the way that society portrays the homeless and conceptualizes homelessness should better enable the homeless and their supporters to counter derogatory stereotypes and to challenge oppressive structural arrangements and institutions. Therefore, I work to promote a greater awareness of how the homeless have been portrayed in debate over benchmark federal legislation to aid the homeless in chapter 3. Specifically, a critical legislative history of the Stewart B. McKinney Homeless Assistance Act of 1987—hereafter referred to as "the McKinney Act"—and debate related to its passage and initial re-authorizations is offered as a case study. This work is important since the McKinney Act serves as the foundation for contemporary federal legislation on homelessness and for much contemporary homeless relief and assistance.

Based upon this reading of the McKinney Act and related literature, I identify and label three general perspectives toward homelessness that appear to dominate and circumscribe consideration of homeless people and policy addressing homelessness: the Conservative view, the Educator view, and the Liberal view. I suggest that these perspectives roughly correspond to different regimes of truth.

Awareness of historical origins and a deep historical contextualization of these regimes of truth should further enable the homeless and their supporters to work more effectively for new, more benign social constructions and portrayals of the homeless. Accordingly, in chapter 4 I present a critical historical reconstruction of how each of these regimes of truth rose to prominence as evidenced by their premises serving as the basis for widespread public policies. In particular, I trace the development of English Vagrancy laws from the fourteenth century to the seventeenth centuries in order to highlight the antecedent to today's Conservative stance. I follow the institutionalization of alms-houses in the U.S. in order to illustrate the forerunner of today's Educators stance. Then I sketch the passage of New Deal legislation in order to demonstrate the precursor of today's Liberal stance. Throughout this analysis, I call attention to the integral role that work/labor plays in supporting these regimes of truth and in framing consideration of homelessness today.

In chapter 5 I present a detailed analysis of the way that science as an ideograph and scientific discourse affect the design of public policies addressing homelessness. First, I examine how science is rhetorically employed in political debate concerning homelessness and how science changes the scope of that debate. Next, I look at the historical precedents of contemporary social science and trace how this earlier scientific knowledge influences contemporary debate. Finally, I discuss the way that science as an ideograph delimits reasonable discussion of homelessness.

In chapter 6 I recap my findings and discuss their implications. In particular, I consider how we might make better use of rhetoric to undermine our society's uncritical acceptance of homelessness, poverty, and the economic status quo. I also discuss the problems of looking for a solution to homelessness independent of looking for an overall solution to poverty. Finally, I offer a critical self-appraisal of my analysis in terms of the criteria developed in my discussion of a critical theory approach to the study of homelessness.

Chapter Two
Analytical Perspectives

Language is politics, politics assigns power, power governs how people talk and how they are understood. (Robin Tolmach Lakoff, 1990, p. 6)

Categories are human mental constructs. . . . Policy is centrally about classification and differentiation, about how we do and should categorize in a world where categories are not given. . . . (Deborah A. Stone, reprinted in Babst, 1996, p. 5)

The vocabulary of poverty impoverishes political imagination. For two centuries of American History, considerations of productivity, cost, and eligibility have channeled discourse about need, entitlement, and justice within narrow limits bounded by the market. In every era, a few people have counterposed dignity, community, and equality as standards for policy. But they have remained outsiders, unable to divert powerful currents constraining the possibilities for social thought and action. (Michael B. Katz, 1989, p. 3)

Underlying my application of critical theory to homelessness are three related analytical perspectives: social constructionism, the operation of language, and rhetorical analysis. In particular, chapter 3 highlights the way that the homeless in general and various subgroups of homeless people are socially constructed in the McKinney Act, in related legislation, and in debate about the homeless leading up to the McKinney Act's passage. In addition, the way that the indigent and homeless are socially constructed in earlier public policies are examined in chapter 4.

In chapters 4 and 5, I illustrate the way that notions of homelessness, work, and science play a key role in shaping consideration of homelessness. I do this by presenting an extended historical analysis of the rhetoric employed in discussion of poverty, vagrancy, and homelessness. In chapter

5, I also discuss the way that science as a narrative affects contemporary society.

Underpinning each of these chapters is an awareness of the workings of language. Indeed, specific examples of how language operates in reproducing certain uncritical views of homelessness are illustrated in chapters 3, 4 and 5.

Accordingly, each of these perspectives merits discussion before I begin my analysis. As suggested in chapter 1, I have prepared this book with the four minimum criteria of a critical theory in mind. Attention to the third criterion—that the critical theory should be made intelligible to readers—requires that I avoid using excessive jargon. It further demands that I must explain and define any jargon that I do use so that my work remains accessible to readers. Therefore, in this chapter I present a brief discussion of social constructionism, reification, myth, differentiation, the logic of identity, ideographs, narratives and characterizations.

SOCIAL CONSTRUCTIONISM

The social constructionist perspective provides a useful way to analyze various portrayals and images associated with homelessness (e.g., see Berger & Luckmann, 1966; Spector & Kitsuse, 1977). In particular, the contextualist school of the social constructionist movement (e.g., see Best, 1995) nicely compliments the ideographic perspective discussed later in this chapter. The social constructionist perspective stands in contrast to more traditional social science approaches to the study of social problems such as homelessness. Social scientists typically presume that social problems exist as objective conditions or arrangements within society. These objective conditions or arrangements are viewed as intrinsically harmful to a normal or healthy society. Herbert Blumer explains that for social scientists who subscribe to this view, their key task

> is to identify the harmful condition or arrangement and to resolve it
> into its essential elements or parts. This analysis of the objective
> makeup of the social problem is usually accompanied by an identifica-
> tion of the conditions which cause the problem and by proposals as to
> how the problem might be handled. In having analyzed the objective
> nature of the social problem, identified its causes, and pointed out how
> the problem could be handled or solved the sociologist believes that he
> [sic] has accomplished his scientific mission. (1971, p. 298)

However, the social constructionist perspective assumes that the social construction of knowledge, ideas, categories, and appropriate social relations is responsible for creating and/or fermenting social problems—in large or small part depending on the particular social constructionist theory one ascribes to.

For the most radical of the social constructionists, all reality is discursively constructed (e.g., see Pfhol, 1985; Fish, 1989). They hold that while there may be a reality outside of language, we can know nothing of it because all perceptions are filtered through language. Rosenau writes that for those who hold this position, "Reality is the result of the social processes accepted as normal in a specific context" (1992, p. 111). In the sociological literature, those accepting this perspective are known as strict constructionists. Joel Best writes:

> In their view, constructionists should examine the perspectives of claimsmakers, policymakers, and other members of society. The actual social conditions are irrelevant; what matters is what the members say about those conditions. . . . In fact, because they adopt a phenomenological perspective, strict constructionists question the analyst's ability to make judgements about social conditions. Phenomenological sociology argues that all we know about the world is a social construction. This includes the claims members make about social issues, but it also includes the analyses that constructionist sociologists write about claimsmaking. (1995, pp. 341–342)

Accordingly, strict constructionists might be said to view language and discourse as more material than material reality itself (cf. McGee, 1982).

Those most diametrically opposed to this view maintain that there is always a clearly delineated physical world independent of, yet knowable through, language. This position underlies the traditional social science approach outlined above and popular notions of science as discussed in chapter 5. The most strident adherents of this view accept a correspondence theory of language; a theory that there is an exact one-to-one correspondence between the word or symbol (signifier) and the object, concept or thing (signified). As suggested earlier, language is thought merely to be a simple, straightforward naming process (Saussure, 1989, p. 3). Because of this, such proponents hold that language can serve as a neutral medium for observing reality.

Both of these positions are extreme and seemingly few scholars hold one or the other. In fact, one might be hard pressed to identify any contemporary scholar who admits to accepting the traditional social science perspective outlined above. Between these two extremes lies a myriad of alternative positions that may be placed along a continuum ranging from total construction of reality to complete correspondence between signifier and signified. In terms of this continuum, I hold an intermediary view of social constructionism in which there is a reality outside of language, but most, if not all, meaningful experience of that reality is mediated through language.[1] Moreover, just as language shapes our knowledge of reality and relation to it, our conception of reality itself is limited by the properties of that extra-linguistic reality in two ways. First, unmediated reality delimits our linguistic and sensory capabilities. For example, our visual and auditory sensory ranges are extremely limited in comparison to many other species. Second, extra-linguistic reality seems to exhibit physical characteristics that can serve as the basis for truth claims about reality. From this perspective, languages, discourses, and past social constructions have material consequences that in turn affect contemporary and future social constructions.

The verb form of the term "social construction" refers to the social process of defining and organizing reality. Indeed, for Blumer social problems "lie in and are products of a process of collective definition" (1971, p. 301). Further developing this idea, Gordon Babst explains that through social construction, " . . . society defines and organizes a concept or idea, however loosely integrated, . . . ambiguous and inconsistent this organization may be" (1996, p. 9). For example, consider the social construction of target populations. As mentioned earlier and illustrated in greater detail in the next chapter, public policies identify—or target—those who are to receive either benefits or burdens. These recipients may be described as target populations (see Schneider & Ingram, 1994). In presenting target populations, public policies convey messages concerning members of these target populations; e.g., whether they are deserving or undeserving, whether they are laudable or reprehensible. The end product of this process is a social construction (noun form).

Babst writes that "[t]here is nothing inherently stereotypical about a social construction, regardless of the extent to which one or another stereotype may be a building block in a social construction. A social construction refers to a concatenation of factors from a variety of sources, and is not arrived at by independent reason alone" (1996, p. 9). Public policies addressing social ills such as homelessness and poverty are built upon and re-present already extant social constructions, images, discourses and stereotypes (e.g., see Schur, 1965; Schneider & Ingram, 1993; 1997). And they may be instrumental in introducing new ones as well. Because of this, social constructions are also sources of other social constructions.

In essence, policymakers draw from an extant social system to make claims about both physical and social reality. Every social system has its own dominant history, imagery, myths, ideology and notions of gender, race, sexuality, etc. (Gramsci, 1971). Larger social systems also typically have competing histories, literary images, narratives and notions of gender, race, ethnicity, sexuality, and the like. These serve as the building blocks from which policymakers construct public policies.

Accordingly, policies are created and implemented to address socially constructed and therefore, somewhat intangible, problems. But in addressing problems from a certain perspective, in providing benefits and/or burdens to some individuals and groups and not to others, and in demonstrating that some issues are important enough to merit public response, policy also plays a role in socially constructing the very concepts, ideas, and populations upon which it is based.

Schneider and Ingram argue that policies send messages both to those targeted by public policy and to society-at-large by means of the social constructions they employ. They explain: "Even without direct experience with policy, the language and symbols contained in policy send messages about what kind of people count as important, whose interests are likely to be taken seriously and whose problems will likely be ignored" (1997, p. 79). They argue that these messages may be internalized by members of particular target populations and that, having internalized these messages, individuals may act in ways that reinforce these messages. Using the example of the criminalization of deviance, Edwin Schur argues that " . . . the relation between deviance and public policy is reciprocal" (1965, p. 8). He explains:

> The definition of behavior as 'criminal' is an extreme form of stigmatization. Defining behavior as 'deviant' has profound effects on those individuals engaging in it . . . Even when he [sic] is not publicly identified and officially dealt with, he is only too aware that his behavior is legally proscribed as well as socially disapproved. Sensing that he is different or is doing an unusual act is one thing; feeling that his act is strongly disapproved is another; and knowledge that he has become a lawbreaker yet another. (Schur, 1965, p. 5)

This constitutive function of policy is best understood by those already stigmatized or branded as deviants. Consider the example of women's struggle to gain greater reproductive rights. Feminists and their supporters have expended great energy and effort to secure and maintain these rights. While debate is usually framed in terms of legal rights, much more is at stake (cf., Johnson, 1989). At issue is not only the preservation of women's legal rights to have access to abortion and to practice various forms of birth control, but also the status of women as mature adults capable of making informed decisions concerning their bodies and their interests. In terms of Schneider and Ingram's position, their status as full citizens, as people whose interests are taken seriously, and who are important and powerful, is on the line.

OPERATIONS OF LANGUAGE

As discussed above, postmodern critical theorists are highly suspicious of foundational conceptions of reality. For such critics, publicly challenging grand narratives or meta-narratives is a primary (political) undertaking. Accordingly, critical scholars engaged in such political work frequently discuss language's operation in terms of reification, myth, differentiation, and the logic of identity.

Generally speaking, critics strategically confront correspondence theories of language (Eagleton, 1983) by performing deconstructions of them and by rendering genealogical accounts of institutions and disciplines (e.g., see Derrida, 1974; cf. Jay, 1992). As an example, critics ranging from Emile Durkheim to Jacques Derrida have been concerned with the way that abnormality is used unreflectively to distinguish what is normal. Unfortunately, concern over uncritical use of the normal/abnormal dichotomy is clearly warranted given recent genocidal practices in Rwanda, Sudan, and the Balkans and given the increasing number of hate crimes committed against members of minority groups in the U.S. and Europe. Closer to home, the Southern Poverty Law Center reports that the number of hate groups operating in the U.S. has risen significantly over the last decade. In 1997 it documented the existence of 474 hate groups in the U.S. and warned of the alarming increase of such groups that year (1998, p. 6). Six years later it documented the existence of 751 hate groups (Southern Poverty Law Center, 2003).

In regards to the case of the homeless, many advocates for the homeless work hard to overcome the stigmatization attached to homelessness. (This is discussed in greater detail in the next chapter.) The homeless have been and continue to be presented as "just like the rest of us," as "ordinary people," or as "people you know" who happen to have no place to live through no fault of their own (see Baum & Burnes, 1993, pp. 124–6).[2] Notice that even in the attempt to overcome negative stereotyping in this way, notions of normalcy and the ordinary are relied upon. The strategy of associating the homeless with "us" seems to work because people who view themselves as normal typically view themselves as deserving, too. But apparently not everyone is deserving. If everyone were deserving, then there would be no need to take note that the homeless are "just like the rest of us." Therefore, those who are clearly not "just like the rest of us" may appear as undeserving.

Furthermore, this clear divide, between "we" ordinary folk who have homes and our unfortunate brethren, the homeless, fosters the idea that there is a clearly delineated normal state of having a home—"homedness" perhaps. In this way, having a home is made to appear as a static or inherent quality, not a contingent social arrangement. As William Connolly explains: "A theory of the normal individual establishes its parameters of normality not so much by . . . argumentation as by omissions in its generic characterization of the individual" (1991, p. 74). Such omissions are cause for concern since this denial of the particular and the individual facilitates the invisibility of some. As only one example, feminists of color and lesbian and bi-sexual feminists argue that the feminism of the 1960s and 1970s was all too White, academic, and middle class (e.g., hooks, 1981). By presenting women as a unified whole in the fight for equal rights, the experiences and needs of many, perhaps most, women went unacknowledged.

This situation offers evidence of reification at work. Through reification, the existence of a certain kind of thing or type of person is posited but not explained.[3] The social relations that underlie these things or types are presented in such a way that they appear to be beyond human control.

Returning to the example of the homeless, they are posited in contrast to those with homes and with the affluent. Etymologically speaking, there can be no homeless without the prior existence of "homed." In this way, the homeless are a derivative of those with homes. Thus, the "homed" and the homeless are presented as real, substantive beings whose independent existence is a given. Presented in this way, it is easy to miss the social relations that underlie having a home in which to live.

For example, housing is not typically thought of as a human right in the U.S. but it is in some countries (e.g., decent housing is guaranteed to all Cubans in Cuba's constitution). These differences lead to very different policies and perspectives toward housing. Furthermore, private property relations and inheritance, mainstays of the U.S. social and political systems, result in a particular distribution of homes. Countries not founded upon these institutions develop other patterns of home distribution. But by presenting those with and without homes as substantive beings in their own right without reference to these and other contingent and malleable social relations, these relations appear fixed, necessary, and ahistorical.

Yet one may reasonably ask, in an economic system where full employment permits around five percent of the total eligible, able-bodied workforce to be out of work, why should housing be tied to one's ability to find work? Similarly, one may reasonably ask, in a country as culturally diverse as the United States, why should housing be tied to behaving in accordance with middle-class values and social mores? Yet such questions are not asked as frequently as they might be. Moreover, when they are asked, they do not carry the weight they might due to the workings of reification—after all, for many it seems that the homeless and "homed" have always been with us.

In contrast, some critical theorists emphasize the process by which the meaning of any particular expression derives its significance in relational contrast to other expressions (i.e., differentiation) in their work to challenge oppression. Anything that is identifiable necessarily presupposes something else against which the thing is distinguished. However, this something else is also identified in relation to another presupposed something else, and so on, *ad infinitum*. In effect, meaning is the product of terms or symbols (signifiers), not the thing referred to by the term or symbol (signified). Taking Saussure's linguistic theory to its logical conclusion, Derrida describes language as a process of unending slippage of meaning. He coined the term "différance" to describe this process. From this perspective, language is a system of negative differences without positive terms. However, the idea or appearance of presence or substantive being is one of the products of differentiation or différance. Many critical theorists argue that differentiation is fundamental to the operation of language (e.g., see Derrida, 1981; Norris, 1982; Baudrillard, 1983b). Such critics argue that because the vast majority of conscious experience of the world, if not all conscious experience, is mediated through language, differentiation underlies all meaningful human social relations.

In spite of this unending deferral of meaning, the sense of presence arising as a result of differentiation is more commonly conceptualized in terms of dichotomous pairings rather than in terms of multiple groupings or continua. In fact, social scientists typically use continua in their work rather than definite categories. However, this is not usually the case for society-at-large. For example, in everyday life, the term "rich" is usually juxtaposed with poor, not middle class, ultra rich, working class or some combination of these, even though this is certainly a possibility. Dichotomies often have a positively valued category that sustains its value at the expense of the other category (cf. Lakoff & Johnson, 1980). It is by this process that one category is devalued at the expense of another that one becomes a negative Other (cf. Kyle, 2001b).

To use a recurring theme in American culture as an example, some people assume that in the natural order of things, individual merit underlies personal achievement. Therefore, one can speak of the deserving and the undeserving in absolute terms. When used as a filter for viewing individual fortune and achievement, those individuals who are more successful (certainly the "homed") are more valued than those who are less successful—clearly the homeless. The presentation of such dichotomous relationships without explaining the underlying moves making these dichotomies possible bolsters an unproblematic view of these and similar social relations.

Moreover, postmodern critical theorists have discussed how the abstract conceptualization of universal categories and the defining characteristics that are inherent in such dichotomous thinking deny difference and the particular (Connell, 1992; Young, 1990b). For example, Iris Young critically explains how the logic of identity (or in Derrida's terms, "the metaphysics of presence") can be oppressive. She argues that things are presented in terms of substance rather than in terms of process or interrelatedness. Phenomenological experience is ordered so that particular experiences are comparable. She writes:

> Reason seeks essence, a single formula that classifies concrete particulars as inside or outside a category, something common to all things that belong in the category. The logic of identity tends to conceptualize entities in terms of substance rather than process or relation; substance is the self-same entity that underlies change, that can be identified, counted, measured. . . . [the logic of identity] constructs totalizing systems in which the unifying categories are themselves unified under principles, where the ideal is to reduce everything to one first principle. (Young, 1990b, p. 98)

In doing so, abstract conceptualization allows and/or sustains oppression.

As a more concrete, though oversimplified, example, such dichotomous and categorical thinking facilitates the marking of financial failure or the failure to exhibit one's wealth as abnormal. In Social Darwinian terms, it allows the labeling of individuals who do not exhibit signs of social wealth and success as "the weak." It facilitates the recognition of those without permanent homes—perhaps the most easily identifiable of the weak—as a sub or minority group known as the homeless. Therefore, it facilitates the consignment of those identified as the homeless to the ranks of deviant, or at best, to the ranks of dependent. Through the logic of identity, the homeless are conceptualized as one-dimensional. The experiences and social, cultural, and economic relations that shape and define individuals who experience homelessness are obscured. The homeless exist only as homeless. And as homeless, they are assigned the qualities the homeless are expected to have; as seen in this example, weakness. This has important consequences for those without homes that go beyond living with a negative label or being stereotyped. Consider that even when public policies are created to address their needs, it is typically non-profit and government agencies and their employees who receive direct benefits in terms of cash payments (salaries), not those without homes themselves (Schneider & Ingram, 1997).

Recognition of reification, myth, differentiation, and the logic of identity leads postmodern critical theorists to posit a view of the self that radically conflicts with the Enlightenment portrayal of the self as an autonomous agent existing prior to language and thus free to employ language as a simple tool (cf. Foucault in Simons, 1995, p. 47). Such critics argue that for humans, the conceivable is already inscribed in the discourses and histories that have preceded them. Barthes explains that "there is no reality not already classified by men [sic]: to be born is nothing but to find this code ready-made and to be obliged to accommodate oneself to it" (1972a, p. xvii). Indeed, T. Minh-ha Trinh writes of the constraints experienced by Others: "Language is one of the most complex forms of subjugation, being at the same time the locus of power and unconscious servility. With each sign that gives language its shape lies a stereotype of which I/I am both the manipulator and the manipulated" (1989, p. 52).

RHETORICAL ANALYSIS

In chapters 4 and 5, I concentrate on the role that three particular terms (homelessness, work and science) play in facilitating and replicating poverty and homelessness. But I suggest that these terms function as more than just terms or signifiers. They function as what a number of communication scholars have termed "ideographs." In addition, in chapter 5 I argue that science may be viewed as a narrative that plays a constitutive part in the creation of our society's dominant ideology, or from the perspective of postmodern critical theorists, its role in the creation of the Enlightenment meta-narrative.

Ideographs

A number of scholars have advanced the notion of the ideograph as a unit of analysis for the study of political rhetoric (McGee, 1975; 1980a; 1980b; McGee & Martin, 1983; Condit, 1987; Hasian, 1996; Kyle, 2001a). They argue that ideographs play a crucial role in shaping and constraining political debate. Celeste Condit (1987, p. 3) describes the concept of the ideograph as a needed attempt to marry the symbolic interactionist and the materialist approaches to the study of language. This marriage is premised on a particular understanding of social control. As Michael McGee explains, social control involves control over consciousness through learned predispositions. He writes: "Human beings are 'conditioned,' not directly to belief and behavior, but to a vocabulary of concepts that function as guides, warrants, reasons, or excuses for behavior or belief" (1980a, pp. 5–6). Those vocabulary terms identified as ideographs function as a priori influences over our understandings of appropriate behavior. Accordingly, we tend to limit ourselves or at least to react in similar ways when we encounter certain terms. As McGee suggests, ideographs appear to have some *intrinsic force* to compel rational agreement just by their usage.

> Though words only, and not claims, these terms are more pregnant than declarative sentences could be. They are the building-blocks of 'ideology.' We might think of them as 'ideographs,' for like Chinese symbols, they signify and 'contain' a unique ideological commitment; further, they presumptuously suggest that each member of our community will see as a *gestalt* every complex nuance in them. (McGee, 1980b, p. 74)

In effect, the ideographs themselves typically are not subjected to serious contemplation since we are all expected to have a common understanding of the term. This presumption on the part of those who both actively and passively accept ideographs effectively directs discussion and critical engagement away from the ideograph's own uncertain foundation. In this way, ideographs set *some* of the boundaries of reasonable debate. While in actuality there is no ahistorical or universal meaning to these terms, the universality of these terms is widely anticipated. In McGee's words:

> An ideograph is an ordinary-language term found in political discourse. It is a high-order abstraction representing collective commitment to a particular but equivocal and ill-defined normative goal. It warrants the use of power, excuses behavior and belief which might otherwise be perceived as eccentric or antisocial, and guides behavior and belief into channels easily recognized by a community as acceptable and laudable (1980a, p.15).

In this way, the notion of ideograph appears consistent with the social constructionist perspective.

Therefore, as evidenced in the next chapter, the role that ideographs such as work and science play in warranting particular policies addressing homelessness merit empirical analysis. In fact, Marouf Hasian, Jr., suggests: "The importance of ideographic analysis comes from its empirical approach which attends to the way that a public actually voiced its concerns over an issue rather than looking for the ways that the 'masses' failed to live up to some rational standard" (1996, p. 8).

The meaning of an ideograph is established by using the term as a description of a particular phenomenon; like language in general, an ideograph "has meaning only insofar as our description is acceptable, believable" (McGee, 1980a, p. 10). In order to make a case for, or to define, a particular ideograph, we must make reference to its history by recounting the situations for which the term has appeared to be an appropriate description. "Then by comparison over time, we establish an analog for the proposed present usage of the term. Earlier usages become precedent, touchstones for judging the propriety of the ideograph in a current circumstance" (McGee, 1980a, p. 10). As Condit explains, "An ideograph . . . is *not* an idea (a content disembodied from any form); it is precisely a particular constellation of usages, identifiable solely by the specific forms it takes in past history and the present historical moment" (1990, p. 332). Therefore, the appropriate manner to study an ideograph is through extended historical review of the multiple usages of the term. However, such a review would include not only the more popular or successful employments of the ideograph, but also the dissonant or resistant usages of the ideograph. Furthermore, it would explore the contexts in which these various usages were developed and pursued.[4]

Narratives and Characterizations

While acknowledging the importance of ideographs for the study of political rhetoric, Condit argues that narratives and characterizations also play a significant role in the shaping of rhetorical and material reality (1987, p. 3; see also Fisher, 1984). As suggested earlier, I will argue that science plays an important role as both an ideograph and as a narrative in perpetuating society's dominant ideology or meta-narrative.

Hasian defines narratives as:

> stories that are used in the formation of ideologies. Narratives are different from ideographs in form and function. While ideographs are single, highly evocative words, narratives consist of more elaborate story forms with structured plots. Narratives are accounts of deeds or actions that are meant to be constantly retold. Social actors identify themselves with particular collectives by choosing between competing stories. (1996, p. 160)

Similarly, Condit writes that political narratives arise "when a narrative, through constant retelling, gains pervasiveness and force among an active plurality of persons in a national discourse group. These stories may be true or false by some external standard, but for their audience, they are potent—useful and forceful" (1987, p. 4). As an example, the shock and disbelief of many Americans following the terrorist attacks of 9/11 and the refusal of many Americans even to consider the possibility that the U.S. has any culpability for the events suggests that such thoughts are incompatible with some commonplace U.S. political narratives.

According to one such narrative, the U.S. was founded by immigrants seeking freedom and the means to better themselves. These immigrants and their descendants carved a nation out of a wilderness and in the process they brought freedom, civilization, and progress to much of North America and to other parts of the world. In keeping with its manifest destiny, the nation they built ended European imperialist designs in the hemisphere, and it has been a defender of national self-determination. Thus, the U.S. is a champion of democracy, a shining example of freedom, liberty, and success; indeed, it is a secular version of an earlier day's shining city on a hill (see Kyle, 2001b; cf. Kyle & Angelique, 2002). Hence, the U.S. could not have done anything to elicit these attacks.

Finally, both Hasian and Condit agree that characterizations underpin narratives. Condit suggests that characterizations are the "universalized descriptions of particular agents, acts, scenes, purposes or agencies which when they become culturally accepted as accurate depictions of a class, can be labeled 'character-types'" (1987, p. 4). Hasian concurs with Condit's position and adds that "for the purposes of rhetoric, the importance of a characterization is not necessarily its truth or falsity according to some standard outside of the narrative but rather the potency of the characterization to audiences who identify with particular stories" (1996, p. 160).

Chapter Three
The McKinney Act of 1987

Once again it is the same notion that if you are well-intended enough, you really do not have to worry about the potential results nor the lack of creativity of your plan. All you have to do is spend more money, and somehow you have eased your conscience. . . . (U.S. Representative Pat Swindall speaking on the House floor, reprinted in Fessler & Elving, 1987, p. 1452)

James H. Quillen, R-Tenn., suggested that expanding federal aid to the homeless might encourage more people to join their ranks. 'I don't want the Congress to create more homelessness on our streets,' Quillen said. 'Instead of solving the problem, we would make it entirely more complicated.' (Blakely, 1987, p. 422)

So my appeal to the Members would be to vote no on this bill and send a message to the country that we are ready to stand up and be heard. Let us go back to the work ethic in our country that teaches us to work and earn our living. There is going to be rich, there is going to be poor, and there is going to be middle class. If we do not have that, we are going to be a socialist country, and I think it is time that we stand up and be heard. (U.S. Representative Clyde Holloway speaking to the House during debate on the McKinney Act of 1987).

In this chapter I conduct a critical analysis of a number of texts associated with the debate over the landmark federal legislation on homeless, the McKinney Act of 1987; legislation that still frames contemporary homeless policy. I do so to promote a greater awareness of the rhetorical and discursive forces at play in contemporary society's views of homelessness. Such awareness may aid those identified as homeless to recognize negative social constructions of themselves appearing in public policies and derogatory stereotypes circulating in society-at-large. Once social constructions and those stereotypes are recognized as political portrayals and not as inherent qualities, the homeless and their allies may begin to challenge them strategically. Moreover, they may even begin to work on ways to challenge society to look beyond the rhetoric and to address those institutions and arrangements that facilitate their homelessness. Thus, this analysis furthers the aims of a critical theory of homelessness as discussed earlier.

First, I situate my discussion of the predominant notions of homelessness circulating during the decade immediately preceding the McKinney Act's passage and in the first few years following its passage by presenting a partial legislative history of the McKinney Act. Second, I consider the growing attention to homelessness that occurred over the course of the 1980s leading to its eventual recognition as national crisis. In particular, I examine the role that the popular and academic presses played in facilitating this realization; I present some of the more commonplace portrayals of homeless persons in circulation at the time; and I highlight some strategies employed by advocates for the homeless. Third, I look at the way that the McKinney Act itself portrays the homeless. I report on the way the legislation divides the homeless into types (sub-target populations), and I point out some of the McKinney Act's subtle (and not-so-subtle) messages concerning the dependency and even irresponsibility of the homeless. Finally, I discuss a number of themes permeating discussion of homelessness as presented in the previous sections—themes meriting further consideration in later chapters. In particular, I point out that three general perspectives concerning the homeless appeared repeatedly in debate concerning the McKinney Act and its initial amendments. Therefore, I briefly characterize these perspectives and present the underlying assumptions of each. In addition, I point out that science plays an important role in framing consideration of the homeless. In effect, science is typically presented as the legitimate and appropriate source of knowledge about the homeless. As such, science serves as the backdrop against which rhetorical claims, social constructions, and literary portrayals concerning the homeless are made and illuminated.

LEGISLATIVE OVERVIEW

The McKinney Act (Public Law 100–77) was signed into law by a reluctant Ronald Reagan on July 22, 1987 (National Coalition for the Homeless, 1999). It was first amended on September 30, 1988. The law was presented by lawmakers as an emergency relief effort requiring additional legislation to address the underlying causes of homelessness (e.g., see Gore 1987; 1990). The McKinney Act authorized $1.47 billion in emergency aid for homeless relief, although only $718 million was actually appropriated before the original act expired.[1] Nevertheless, the McKinney Act was the federal government's first major fiscal response to homelessness.

However, it was not the federal government's first response. Besides holding a number of congressional hearings on homelessness, the Federal Interagency Task Force on Food and Shelter for Homeless was established under the department of Health and Human Services in 1983. Its mission was:

> to identify existing resources that can be targeted more effectively towards the needs of the homeless; identify and remove red tape and other impediments to the use of those resources; act as a facilitator in making these resources available to local governments and food and/or shelter providers; serve as an information source on homeless issues; and assist in identifying examples of successful local approaches to homelessness that can be useful to others. (reprinted in FEMA, 1986)

In addition, the federal government appropriated $140 million in 1983 and $70 million in 1984 for emergency food and shelter assistance (reported in Foscarinis, 1996a, p. 161). In May 1984, the Department of Housing and Urban Development released its study, "A Report to the Secretary on the Homeless and Emergency Shelters." In 1986, the government passed the Homeless Eligibility Clarification Act (Public Law 99–570) to remove barriers in existing laws that prevented homeless persons from participating in a number of federal aid programs.

In addition, a number of federal programs specifically addressing various aspects of homelessness were already in place prior to the McKinney Act's passage. The Homeless Housing Act of 1986 (Public Law 99–500) established the Emergency Shelter Grant program and a transitional housing demonstration program. The State Comprehensive Mental Health Services Plan of 1986 (Public Law 99–660) funded the Demonstration Projects for Services for Homeless Chronically Mentally Ill Individuals program. Similarly, funds from the Community Services Block Grant program, authorized under the Human Services Reauthorization Act of 1986 (Public Law 99–425), were available for initiatives affecting "homeless families" (100STAT.969).

As an omnibus law, the McKinney Act brought some of these programs together under its mandate and created a number of new programs as well; yet it was not all-inclusive since some programs affecting the homeless remained outside of its jurisdiction.[2] Nevertheless, the McKinney Act was a broad response to the homeless crisis. It included the establishment and/or extension of over 20 different programs and initiatives under the supervision of seven different federal agencies: Housing and Urban Development (HUD), Heath and Human Services (HHS), Department of Agriculture (DOA), Department of Education (DOE), Department of Labor (DOL), Federal Emergency Management Agency (FEMA), Veterans Administration (VA), and the newly created Interagency Council of the Homeless (ICH). In all, it established 15 new federally funded programs and modified seven programs to better meet the needs of the homeless (Foscarinis, 1996a, 160).

Substantial parts of the act were reauthorized for two years on November 7, 1988, in the Stewart B. McKinney Homeless Assistance Amendments Act of 1988 (Public Law 100–628). During the administration of George H. W. Bush, numerous McKinney Act programs were again amended and reauthorized. For example, the Stewart B. McKinney Homeless Assistance Amendments Act of 1990 (Public Law 101–645) was passed on November 29, 1990. However, while these acts bore the McKinney name in their popular titles, they were not the sole location for McKinney Act legislation. A number of other McKinney Act amendments, programs, and reauthorizations—often addressing the needs of specific subgroups of the homeless—were included in other companion legislation. For example, the Veterans Mentally Ill Program, located in the Veterans's Benefits and Services Act of 1988 (Public Law 100–322) and the Veterans Domiciliary Care Program, found in the Supplemental Appropriations Act of 1987 (Public Law 100–71), focused specifically on the needs of homeless veterans. Similarly, the Runaway and Homeless Youth Program, part of the Anti Drug Abuse Act of 1988 (Public Law 100–690), and the Family Reunification program, authorized in the Cranston-Gonzalez National Affordable Housing Act of 1990 (Public Law 101–625, see Adler 1991:16) were directed at needs of homeless youth and homeless families.

The Stewart B. McKinney Homeless Housing Assistance Amendments Act of 1992 (Public Law 102–550) was passed on October 28, 1992. Like its predecessors, this act was not all-inclusive of federal homeless policy. During the same legislative session, federal lawmakers also approved companion initiatives addressing the needs of various underserved populations. For example, programs directed at homeless children and veterans were passed as separate statutes: the Homeless Children's Assistance Act of 1992 (Public Law 102–512) and the Homeless Veterans Comprehensive Service Programs Act of 1992 (Public Law 102–590).

During the Clinton administration, McKinney Act programs and new programs addressing homelessness appeared in a wide range of federal statutes. For example, the DOE's Adult Education program and its Education for Homeless Children and Youth program from the original McKinney Act and HHS's Family Support Center program from the 1990 McKinney reauthorization were included in the Improving America's Schools Act of 1994 (Public Law 103–382). As another example, renewed funding for the DOL's Job Training for the Homeless Demonstration program, an original McKinney Act program, was included with the School-to-Work Opportunities Act of 1994 (Public Law 130–239).

Each new reauthorization of the McKinney Act saw substantive changes. Some programs were modified or replaced to address previously unmet needs (National Coalition for the Homeless 1999). For example, the original HHS Mental Health Block Grant program was replaced in the 1990 reauthorization (Public Law 101–645) with the Projects for Assistance in Transition from Homelessness program (104STAT.4726). This new program differed from the previous program in that it *required* grant recipients to provide alcohol, and drug-treatment services to those chronically mentally ill clients with substance-abuse problems.

In addition, entirely new programs were developed to address previously unmet needs of selected subgroups of the homeless. For example, the reauthorization of 1990 (Public Law 101–645) established the HHS's Primary Heath Services for Homeless Children program. Its purpose was to provide funds for comprehensive health care services for homeless children and children at imminent risk of becoming homeless (Adler, 1991, p. 25). Similarly, HHS's Homelessness Prevention Demonstration Programs— Family Support Centers and Gateway programs—were initiated in the same reauthorization to provide support to residents of public housing projects at risk of becoming homeless.

And as seen earlier, new programs were created to address the needs of previously unacknowledged subgroups of the homeless. For example, HUD's Housing Opportunities for Persons with AIDS Program (Public Law 101–625) was established in 1991 to assist low-income persons with AIDS. Through this program funds were provided for homelessness prevention activities such as rental assistance and for expenses incurred in the operation of shelters for homeless persons with AIDS (Adler, 1991, pp. 16–17).

There were also changes in funding priorities as the McKinney Act was reauthorized and amended. Besides the creation of new homeless programs and the expansion of others, some programs had their funding cut and some programs were eliminated altogether. For example, the Interagency Council on Homeless (ICH) saw its funding completely eliminated in fiscal year 1994 as it was folded into the White House's Domestic Policy

FIGURE 3.1 • *Federal Expenditures for Homeless Programs: The Stewart B. McKinney Act of 1987 and Subsequent Reauthorizations through 1997**

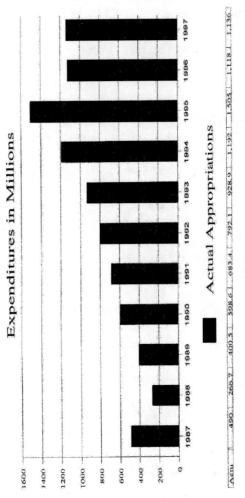

Expenditures in Millions

Actual Appropriations

Actu...	490	265.7	400.5	528.6	683.4	792.1	928.9	1,122	1,505	1,118	1,136
	1987	1988	1989	1990	1991	1992	1993	1994	1995	1996	1997

* Source for actual appropriations data comes from the Interagency Council on Homeless's figure, "McKinney Homeless Funding Levels" provided by George Ferguson during an interview conducted September 3, 1997. Data were compiled February 6, 1997.

Council (see Foscarinis, 1996a, p. 170). Since that time, the ICH has maintained offices in HUD. In addition, HUD has also made legal and administrative services available to the ICH.[3]

Nonetheless, throughout the 1980s and early 1990s, overall funding for McKinney Act programs, for the most part, grew over time. However, despite the elder President Bush's pledge to fully fund McKinney Act programs, appropriations never equaled authorizations. After an initial decline in appropriations from 1987 to 1988, funding gradually increased so that 1990 appropriations exceeded those of 1987. Actual appropriations continued to increase until 1996, when appropriations declined. Figure 3.1 graphically presents the federal funding between 1987 and 1997. While spending for 1997 increased slightly over 1996, once inflation is factored into the equation, funding actually decreased.

GOALS AND JUSTIFICATION

As presented above, the McKinney Act was a broad humanitarian response to the homeless crisis. Its stated goals were:

(1) to establish an Interagency Council on the Homeless;
(2) to use public resources and programs in a more coordinated manner to meet the critically urgent needs of the homeless of the Nation; and
(3) to provide funds for programs to assist the homeless, with special emphasis on elderly persons, handicapped persons, families with children, Native Americans, and veterans (101STAT.485).

But I suggest that the McKinney Act's passage was also a political response designed to relieve perceived political pressure. As Paul A. Toro and Dennis M. McDonnell (1992, p. 54) and many others suggest, there is usually a clear temporal link between public opinion and changes in public policy. The impression of public pressure for homeless relief, whether accurate or not, was brought about by three interrelated occurrences. First, the number of visibly homeless people rose dramatically throughout the 1980s. In addition, the complexion of the homeless appeared to change during the 1980s. Second, there was increased media attention focusing on the homeless situation. Finally, advocates and academicians conscientiously worked to challenge negative characterizations of the homeless by offering more sympathetic characterizations and by increasing public awareness of the plight of people without homes.

THE APPEARANCE OF HOMELESSNESS

There has been, and continues to be, great contention concerning the number of homeless persons. Much of this debate revolves around the soundness and/or appropriateness of the methodological approach used to estimate the number of homeless. Preceding the McKinney Act's passage, numerous studies, reports, and articles focused on this issue. For example, testifying before a U.S. House of Representatives subcommittee on the Urgent Relief for the Homeless Act, Reverend Edwin Conway explained:

> Homelessness, unfortunately, in Chicago is a very serious and worsening problem, for there is no real understanding of the problem. Estimates range from 5 to 25 thousand people who are homeless. There was one scientific study rendered in the course of the last few years, but unfortunately that sampling was very narrow, [sic] restricted it only to the methodology of counting people who were already in shelters. (reprinted in Committee on Banking, 1987, p. 79)

As another example, Carl F. Horowitz greatly contested those who were circulating what he considered to be scientifically unfounded, made-up estimates for the number of homeless. He explained that "such people reject more than 'good data.' They reject the very rational-positivist basis of science–that problem definition precedes solution; that facts precede values; and that means and ends are intimately linked" (1989, p. 69).

Nevertheless, national estimates of the number of homeless on a given night ranged from as high as 3 million, based on Mary Ellen Hombs' and Mitch Snyder's (1982) estimate, to as low as 192,000, based on the low end of HUD's estimate in its *Report to the Secretary on the Homeless and Emergency Shelters* (1984).[4] However, as James D. Wright and Joel A. Devine explained, "By the end of the 1980s, most studies were converging on an X for the nation as a whole in the middle to high hundreds of thousands—somewhere, that is, between 500,000 and 1 million literally homeless people . . . on a typical night" (1992, p. 357).

HUD Secretary Henry G. Cisneros (1993) used the example of Washington, D.C., to illustrate the overall growth of homelessness nationwide. He explained that in 1975, two city-run emergency shelters and the help of several service providers were sufficient to keep up with the basic needs of D.C.'s homeless people. By the end of 1981, the District had fifteen shelters housing 600 people a night; another 200 families received temporary vouchers for hotel and motel rooms each night. Despite the increased assistance, nine homeless people died of exposure that winter. As the problem

Table 3.1: 1988 Estimates of the Number of Homeless Persons in Different Metropolitan Areas

Place	Number Homeless	Place	Number Homeless
Albuquerque	543	Little Rock	300
Atlanta	3,000	Los Angeles	30,000
Baltimore	700	Louisville	620
Baton Rouge	155	Miami	4,500
Birmingham	1,000	Minneapolis	500
Boston	3,000	New York	18,050
Charlotte	255	Philadelphia	2,100
Chicago	3,750	Phoenix	1,155
Cincinnati	925	Pittsburgh	1,500
Cleveland	550	Portland	2,000
Colorado Springs	100	Raleigh	225
Davenport	312	Richmond	350
Dayton	238	Rochester	90
Detroit	5,250	Salt Lake City	489
Fort Wayne	475	San Diego	1,900
Grand Rapids	110	San Francisco	1,670
Hartford	500	Scranton	75
Honolulu	800	Seattle	2,250
Houston	5,000	Syracuse	425
Kansas City	275	Tampa	500
Las Vegas	1,500	Worcester	900

Information originally presened by Deborah Judith Devine, Homelessness and the Social Safety Net (1988), and reproduced in Roleff (1996, p. 29).

continued to worsen, D.C. residents responded in 1984 by approving an initiative guaranteeing everyone the "right to adequate overnight shelter." This entailed a substantial expansion of D.C.'s shelter system. By 1989, D.C. was sheltering more than 11,000 single adults and 2,400 families a year at a cost of over $40 million.

But this dramatic increase in the number of people seeking aid was not limited to Washington, D.C., or even to a particular region of the country. The rise in the number of visible homeless persons was a nationwide phenomena. For example, Table 3.1 presents estimated numbers of homeless persons in different urban areas in 1988.

Such dramatic increases in the number of visibly homeless persons and the widespread distribution of homeless persons did not go unnoticed. Manuel A. Manrique reported that, whereas only 35 percent of Americans claimed that they had personal contact with a homeless person in 1986, 51 percent of Americans claimed that they had had such an experience by 1989 (1994:5). Similarly, Joel Blau wrote, "A 1990 New York Times poll reported that 68 percent of urban Americans see the homeless in the course of their daily routine . . . an 18 percent increase in just four years" (reprinted in Roleff, 1996, p. 12). Regardless of the actual number, the McKinney Act did not overtly address the issue of the number of homeless. However, it did explicitly recognize that homelessness is on the rise (101STAT.484).

In addition to the rising number of homeless, Karen Spar and Monique C. Austin reported that there was a substantive change in the composition of the homeless. In a Congressional Research Service report released in September, 1984, they wrote: "Unlike the skid row 'derelicts' who comprised the typical homeless population of the 1960s, today's street people represent many diverse groups including: the mentally ill, evicted families, the aged, alcoholics, drug addicts, abused spouses, abused young people, and cast-off children" (1984, p. 1). Members of this earlier "typical homeless population" often appear in literary works where they are portrayed as "bums," "tramps," "vagabonds," "hoboes," "hustlers," and "panhandlers." Such images typically elicit images of lazy white men who choose to take advantage of responsible citizens who work for a living—as do popular references to these character types. Accordingly, for many the "typical homeless" of the 1960s and 1970s seem undeserving of sympathy and aid.

As a colorful example, Mike Royko shared the following in his May 24, 1973, column entitled, "Panhandlers' Stories Can Be Refreshing."

> I was glad to see that another imaginative panhandler is working the streets. There aren't many really good ones, at least none in the same class as the legendary Greasy Chin Smith, who used to be seen in the Loop almost every day. He was known as Greasy Chin because he gnawed on a long, old bone to dramatize how poor he was.

> One of the better ones currently at work is an elderly man who stopped me one day and, in an urgent voice, said: 'I'm 67 years old and I must go to Minneapolis.' That's all he said. I don't have any idea what it was supposed to mean, but it sounded so important that I handed him a quarter. I watched him hustle four others before he left for Minneapolis, by way of Elfman's Bar.

> Then there is The Weeper, a kid about 12 who operates on the Near North Side and in the Wrigley Building area. His tear ducts work like windshield washers. When he stops someone and starts blubbering, and the tears flow down his cheeks, it's difficult to figure out what his

problem is, except he needs money. The Weeper is no two-bit moocher, either. He thinks big, howling that his mother and five little brothers and sisters are stuck at a railroad station and they need $ 4.90 to get home. He cornered author Studs Terkel on the street one day and was sobbing so hard, Terkel handed him a dollar. 'That's not enough,' the kid cried. Studs handed him another dollar. 'That's still not enough,' he sobbed. Another dollar. 'Mister, I need more, more,' the kid said, tearing at his hair, so great was his grief. He got Terkel for five dollars. 'I knew he was a moocher,' Terkel said, 'but what a performance!'

Then there is the kid who works the south half of the Loop. He carries an old charity card with holes in it for coins. He points at his ears to indicate deafness and wiggles his fingers in what is meant to be sign language. If you came up behind him and said 'Stickemup,' he'd start running, that's how deaf he is.

Some people get mad when they realize they've been taken in by a phony hard-luck story. Not me. After listening to enough political fund-raising speeches, I find The Weeper almost refreshing. (Royko, 1973)

Royko's rhetorical use of the homeless indicated how wide-spread and accept-able such characterizations of the homeless were at the time. His apparent goal was to satirize political fund-raising. By comparing fund-raisers to these homeless panhandlers, he suggested that fund-raisers are panhandlers too, but perhaps not as good or not as imaginative as the homeless characters he pre-sented. The cleverness and humor of his column are based upon his audience's willingness to accept the homeless caricatures he presented as familiar, even legitimate. He did not describe these panhandlers in great detail. Had he needed to explain or defend his characterizations of the homeless, he would not have been able to effectively poke fun at political fund-raisers.

Review of the McKinney Act itself suggests that the homeless Royko uses in his essay are comprised of those able-bodied, mentally fit, male non-veterans who are not chronic substance abusers. For some, they are "lazy, shiftless bums" or, as former U.S. President Ronald Reagan explained, they are people who are "homeless by choice" (reprinted in Wright, 1989, p. 46). This "typical homeless population" which appeared predominantly throughout the 1960s and 1970s merits greater considera-tion since it played—and continues to play—an important role in ferment-ing and enabling opposition to federal homeless aid and to social welfare programs like Temporary Aid to Needy Families (TANF) generally.

This group did not expressly appear in the McKinney Act and its sub-sequent reauthorizations. However, this should not be surprising. After all, the McKinney Act was primarily a benefit distributing policy. Since "lazy, shiftless bums" are, by definition, responsible for their fate, they are definitely members of a deviant subgroup. In keeping with the work of Schneider and Ingram (1993; 1997), such deviants should be the recipients of burdens, or at least discipline, not benefits. And in fact, despite the McKinney Act's specification of which deserving homeless were to receive benefits and its non-recognition of those easily labeled "lazy, shiftless bums," some opposed the measure because such homeless persons would still be the recipients of benefits. For example, Pamela Fessler and Ronald D. Elving reported that although the Senate adopted the homeless-aid conference agreement, the decision was contested. They wrote: "While the new aid was roundly praised by Democrats and Republicans alike for addressing a national crisis, a few dissenters argued that the legislation merely creates an expensive welfare program that would do little to reduce homelessness" (1987:1452). Similarly, during floor debate on what would become the McKinney Act, Congressman Clyde Holloway declared:

> It is time that we stand together and say, 'Listen, there are 10 million people out there who would love free housing.' I am homeless if you want to look at it that way.

> It is time that we look at it and say, 'What is the role of the Federal Government? What are we to do?'

> There is no end if we are going to keep offering candy bars. There is no end to the line that is going to line up and wait for candy. I think that we have totally lost touch and I hope that we can make a little difference here in Congress. If I cannot, I would much rather be in Louisiana. (1987, p. 1024)

Furthermore, a number of measures designed to modify the behavior of this group of the homeless were offered and debated. Some of these measures are similar to the work requirements that the Personal Responsibility and Work Opportunity Reconciliation Act of 1996 (Public Law 104–193) demands of welfare recipients. In this way, the McKinney Act was a precursor to TANF programs. For example, Stanley Blakely reported that on March 5, 1987, the U.S. House of Representatives approved an amendment to the omnibus homeless bill (HR 558) that would become the McKinney Act. The amendment authorized "local communities with 'workfare' laws *to require able-bodied homeless persons to work for their assistance.* Communities without workfare statutes could institute job-search programs to find work for the homeless" (italics added, Blakely, 1987, p. 423).

The Changing Complexion of Homelessness

Numerous commentators pointed to a concomitant increase in media attention on homelessness during the 1980s and through the first half of the 1990s (White, 1992; Arango, 1995; Roleff, 1996). For example, portrayals of the homeless and homeless characters appeared in popular songs such as Don Henley's *Sunset Grill* (1984), Paul Simon and Lady Smith Black Mambazo's *Homeless* (1986), Phil Collins' *Another Day in Paradise* (1989) and Jewel's *Who Will Save Your Soul* (1994), in Tony Kushner's Pulitzer Prize and Tony Award winning Broadway production, *Angels in America* (1992), and in movies such as *Down and Out in Beverly Hills* (1983), *Trading Places* (1983), *Coming to America* (1988), *Ironweed* (1987) and *The Fisher King* (1991).

There was a corresponding increase in the frequency of news reports concerning the homeless at this time as well. Sung Whang (1993, p. 107) reported that the ABC, NBC and CBS television networks ran a combined total of 358 news items concerning homelessness between 1985 and 1991. This averaged approximately one news report per week on one or the other of the major networks throughout this seven-year period. However, as Whang pointed out, "the number of homeless stories covered during the three month period . . . (November through January) reached almost 50% (174 out of 358) of the total" (1993, p. 105). This averaged approximately two news reports per week on one of the major networks each holiday season throughout this seven-year period. Drawing upon a number of polls, including a nationwide 1988 survey by the National Campaign to End Hunger and Homelessness in America, Michael Dear and Brendan Gleeson explained that of those reports portraying the homeless sympathetically during the 1980's, "the most prominent media message has been that the general public approves of spending more taxes on programs to combat homelessness" (1991, p. 156). Similarly, Manrique (1994, pp. 4–5) reported that opinion polls in the latter 1980s indicated a majority of Americans favored increasing assistance to the homeless.[5]

In addition, advocates and scholars overtly worked to publicize the plight of the homeless (see Rochefort & Cobb, 1993, p. 52). Perhaps the most celebrated or notorious examples of advocates publicizing homelessness revolve around Mitch Snyder's efforts. Not only did he stage media events such as the "Grate American Sleep-Out," but he and Mary Hombs also began circulating a highly questionable, and probably greatly inflated, figure for the number of homeless.[6] In their work, *Homelessness In America: A Forced March to Nowhere* (Hombs & Snyder, 1982), they made the claim that approximately 2.2 million people were homeless in 1980 and they suggested that as many as three million people could become homeless by 1983. Anna Kondratas (1990) argues that this figure, although fabricated, gained wide currency and played a significant role in subsequent debate concerning homeless aid. Similarly, Horowitz wrote:

> Beginning around 1983, the number of three million—approximately 1.2 of every 100 hundred Americans—has come to be reported as the benchmark figure. Politicians, celebrities, and corporations have found it a convenient rallying point to elicit sympathy and tax deductible donations for the homeless. (1989, p. 66)

As he explained, these figures were created precisely for this political purpose. He quoted Snyder testifying before a Joint House Committee in May 1984 to support his position. Snyder testified, "'These numbers [three million homeless] are in fact meaningless. We have tried to satisfy your gnawing curiosity for a number because we are Americans with Western little minds that have to quantify everything in sight, whether we can or not'" (reprinted in Horowitz, 1989, p. 67).

Besides these highly publicized efforts, the number of published works and reports on homelessness produced by academics increased dramatically in the latter 1980s as well. Toro and McDonnell reported that a search of professional literature indexed in *Psychological Abstracts* reveals a dramatic increase in scholarly work on homelessness through the 1980s. They wrote that there were "4 articles on homelessness in 1980, 20 in 1984, 46 in 1988, 175 in 1989, and 265 in 1990. A recent bibliography of books and articles from the past three decades on homelessness contains 488 entries, 285 published since 1985" (1992, pp. 53–54). Indeed, in 1991 the *Journal of Social Distress and the Homeless,* an academic journal devoted to homelessness, began publication and continues to this day.

As Niki L. Young (1994, p. 41) explained, throughout the 1980s and early 1990s the majority of literature on homelessness was produced by advocates who portrayed the homeless sympathetically. Indeed, academicians and advocates for the homeless continue to challenge stereotypes and present the homeless in a sympathetic light (e.g., Hopper, 2003; Williams, 2003). This was in clear contrast to the predominant characterizations of the "typical homeless population" appearing during the 1960s and 1970s. In fact, academicians and advocates referred to "atypical" homeless groups, especially homeless families and homeless mentally ill, so frequently and with such great consistency in official public forums that it seems to have been a strategy—and a successful one at that—employed to garner sympathy for the homeless in general. As an example, Table 3.2 describes the photographic presentation of the homeless appearing in the *Congressional Quarterly* from 1986 through 2004. During this period, only five images accompanied *CQ* articles dealing with homelessness. Moreover, all five images appeared with articles published between March 1987 and June 1988. However, not one of these photographs clearly presents a homeless person consistent with the "typical homeless population" of the 1960s and 1970s.[7] In fact, viewed together as a collective portrayal of the homeless, these pictures suggest that homelessness disproportionately affects African Americans.

Table 3.2: Summary of Pictorial Depictions of the Homeless Appearing in the Congressional Quarterly from 1987 to the 2004

Date of Publication	Picture Subject, Activity and Location [*accompanying caption*]
March 7, 1987*	Disheveled adult of unknown gender and ethnicity, walking along a street away from the camera in ragged clothing with a variety of bags [*The nation's homeless receive new food, health and housing aid.*]
July 4, 1987	Adult African-American male, seated on the ground in front of the White House in the snow wearing a heavy coat and a plastic sheet or tarp around his legs, rubs his hands together for warmth [*Sponsors say homeless individuals can expect more housing, food and health assistance next winter under the two-year measure cleared by Congress.*]
August 6, 1987	Adult African-American male, seated among mattresses, overturned furniture under ceiling of some kind [*The bill would help provide shelter, food, health care, job training and other services for the nation's growing homeless population.*]
May 28, 1988*	Disheveled adult of unknown gender and ethnicity, walking along a street away from the camera in ragged clothing with a variety of bags [*no caption*]
June 25, 1988	A worn and haggard-looking adult African-American man, woman and child, seated in front of bags of clothing and other things, stare warily into the camera [*Last year's budget agreement forced members to decide between funding space exploration and providing money for the homeless and other housing programs.*]

*This photograph reappears on both March 7, 1987 and May 28, 1988.

Consider the U.S. House subcommittee hearing on the Urgent Relief for the Homeless Act of 1987 (H.R. 558) as another example. Throughout this hearing, speaker after speaker pointed out that the homeless are a heterogeneous group. For example, Governor Mario Cuomo testified: "There are more homeless men, women and children—you've heard it now already three times this morning and this is the fourth—more homeless men, women and children in America today than there were at the height of the Great Depression" (reprinted in Committee on Banking, 1987, p. 38). Especially noteworthy are the repeated references to families (see Kyle, 2001a). For example, Congressman Thomas S. Foley, Congressman McKinney, Reverend Edwin Conway, Sister Joan Kirby, Abraham G. Gerges, and Subcommittee Chairman Gonzalez, to name a few, all spoke of homeless families with children during the hearing. As only one concrete example, Governor Cuomo testified, "Some people are shocked to learn—again, as the majority leader pointed out—that the vast majority of today's homeless are families and that the fastest growing group of homeless Americans is children" (reprinted in Urgent, 1987, p. 36). It appears then that the vast majority of the testimony offered at this hearing—and at many other forums as well—was directed at recasting the homeless in more deserving terms by repeatedly presenting sympathetic characterizations.

Still, some representations of the homeless by some homeless supporters were not as flattering as they might have been. For example, the director of a program shelter for the homeless explained:

> Somehow they just never learned what they needed to learn to get along in this world. They have no sense of planning, no sense of reality, responsibility. A lot of them are just impulsive and childish and irresponsible. And it's like they're almost in a state of arrested development. . . . If there was someone, somewhere just to take the time with them and sort of hit them over the head and say, 'hey, obviously this is not working, you know your current life-style is not working, these are the types of things that you're missing out on . . . ,' and really lead them through the process, and teach them . . . They are salvageable. They don't have to be on welfare and they don't have to be homeless. . . . (reprinted in Timmer, 1988, p. 164)

And as the three quotes at the start of the chapter and Congressman Holloway's later remarks indicate, some opponents of aid for the homeless were not convinced that the homeless deserve assistance, let alone sympathy. Jonathan Kozol pointed to the work of politically conservative columnists and social scientists like Charles Krauthammer, George Will, and Charles

Murray, who argued that we should physically separate the homeless from the general public and perhaps even intern them in almshouses (Kozol, 1987, p. 157).

Still more alarming, apparently some citizens expressed outrage over the mere existence of the homeless and some seemed to hold even more extreme positions (cf. Amster, 2003; 2004). As Abraham G. Gerges, former chairperson of the New York City Select Committee for the Homeless recounts: "When I was first made chairman of the committee I went on a very important program, a radio program, and I spoke about homelessness, and there was a call-up. When everybody called up they said get rid of those people, get them jobs, *sterilize them* [italics added] and so forth" (reported in Committee on Banking, 1987, p. 100). Similarly, Peter Marin reported of his experience at a city council meeting in Santa Barbara, California:

> The council was meeting to vote on the repeal of the sleeping ordinances . . . Council members had been pressured into it by the threat of massive demonstrations . . . But this threat that frightened the council enraged the town's citizens. Hundreds of them turned out for the meeting. One by one they filed to the microphone to curse the council and castigate the homeless. Drinking, doping, loitering, panhandling, defecating, urinating, molesting, stealing—the litany went on and on, was repeated over and over, accompanied by fantasies of disaster: the barbarian hordes at the gates, civilization ended. (1987, p. 40)

Indeed, such vehement indignation continued in the decades following the McKinney Act's passage. Responding to David Holthouse's feature story on homeless young people hanging out in Tempe, Arizona, that appeared in the February 25th edition of *New Times* (Holthouse, 1998), a reader responded: "Boo hoo. Guess what I did when I found myself homeless without a high school diploma? I worked for a living. . . . These jackasses aren't handicapped; they're just lazy bums. Literal losers by choice. I hope they all choke on their hemp 'jewelry' and their stinky dogs eat their filthy carcasses" (Hicks, 1998, p. 3).

Nevertheless, instances of politicians openly criticizing the homeless were relatively rare. Niki L. Young explained:

> One reason that President Reagan's assertion that most of the homeless 'lived on the streets by choice' so outraged advocates and is so often cited by them is that it is one of the few expressly anti-homeless messages attributable to a powerful political figure. It may be more expedient for political authorities to pay 'lip service' to the issue of homelessness . . . than to openly show disdain or contempt. (1994, pp. 41–42)

Despite this talk of lip service, the effectiveness of these numerous positive portrayals of the homeless seems unquestionable. The result of these efforts is reflected in the rhetoric of the McKinney Act itself. In particular, the act offered the following rationale for its existence:

> [D]ue to the record increase in homelessness, States, units of local government, and private voluntary organizations have been unable to meet the basic human needs of all of the homeless and, in the absence of greater Federal assistance, will be unable to protect the lives and safety of all homeless in need of assistance; and the Federal Government has a clear responsibility and an existing capacity to fulfill a more effective respect for the human dignity of the homeless. (101STAT.484–5)

Still, notice that it is only with the failure of the state and local governments and of charity organizations to resolve the crises that the federal government was moved to act. This justification addressed criticisms directed against any expansion of federal authority to dependent or deviant target populations—an argument that appears time and again in earlier discussions of federal welfare aid and an argument that will be addressed in greater detail in the next chapter.

THE HOMELESS IN THE MCKINNEY ACT

The division of the homeless into subgroups characterizes a good part of the McKinney Act. The McKinney Act provides benefits to the homeless target population generally, but in doing so it subdivides the overall homeless target population into more narrowly defined sub-target populations. This division enables the creation of more effective policies designed to meet the unique needs of individual groups of the homeless, and it also serves a critical role in legitimizing the policy.

Relative Political Power of the Homeless

Overall, the homeless are a politically weak target population. Furthermore, there is great disparity in the way the homeless as a target population are portrayed. Discussion of the homeless is cast in terms ranging from greatly deserving to completely undeserving. In terms of Schneider's and Ingram's work (1994; 1997), those who view the homeless as deserving present them as a dependent target population while those who view them as undeserving portray them as a deviant target population.

However, all of the homeless sub-populations are presented by the McKinney Act and other federal homeless measures as if the homeless are irresponsible or incapable. Consider the following three examples. First, the statute does not direct agents to make cash payments to the homeless, and in some places it expressly prohibits the distribution of funds directly to the homeless. For example, Title VI, Subtitle B, Section 611 reads: "The Secretary may not make payments under section 521(a) to a State unless the applicant agrees that amounts received pursuant to such section *will not be expended . . . to make cash payments to intended recipients of mental health services* [italics added]" (101STAT.518). Similarly, Title VI, Subtitle A, Section 601 reads: "The Secretary may not . . . make a grant . . . to an applicant unless the applicant agrees that amounts received pursuant to such subsection *will not, directly or through contract, be expended . . . to make cash payments to intended recipients of health services or mental health services* [italics added]" (101STAT.513).

Homeless people who have overcome their homelessness are an exception under certain conditions. Title VI, Subtitle A, Section 611 states: "Any grantee under subsection (a) *may* provide health services through contracts with nonprofit self-help organizations that are established and managed by current and former recipients of mental health services, or substance abuse services, who have been homeless individuals [italics added] . . ." (101STAT.514). The difference between these two examples revolves around two factors: (a) individual versus collective responsibility and (b) mental health and/or substance abuse treatment versus no treatment. The message seems clear. Individual homeless cannot be trusted to care for their own mental and physical health needs. However, if they receive acceptable treatment and are working collectively in a "self-help" association, then and only then may they be allowed to participate in a limited manner.[8] Thus, professionals such as social workers, substance abuse counselors and psychologists are employed to provide services to the homeless. In effect, professionals, not individual homeless persons, are targeted to receive direct benefits in the form of jobs and salaries (cf. Schneider & Ingram, 1997, p. 177).

A politically powerful target population would not as readily be provided benefits in such an overbearing manner. Consider people victimized by floods, earthquakes, tornadoes and other natural disasters; typical recipients of FEMA aid. Members of this target population are given direct aid in the form of cash payments. The government does not discriminate against homeless disaster victims in the manner it does other homeless people. It does not give aid directly to authorized contractors to build their houses, although it could. It does not require that aid recipients receive house selection training, home maintenance classes, or self-help indoctrination from trained professionals before they are allowed to receive payments to rebuild their homes, although it could. And this despite the fact that typically, many made homeless by natural disasters rebuild their homes in the same flood plain, active fault area, or mud slide area where they lost their house.

Second, prior to the McKinney Act's passage, an amendment requiring that *all* homeless persons seeking health care under the provisions of the McKinney Act be tested for AIDS was considered. As Julie Rovner reported in the *Congressional Quarterly,*

> The House handily defeated an attempt to include mandatory testing for acquired immune deficiency syndrome (AIDS) in the homeless relief bill (HR 558) March 5, [1987] but the amendment's author said he was encouraged that 100 colleagues joined him in voting for the measure. . . . The action marked the first time the House has voted on the sensitive issue of mandatory testing for the deadly disease. (1987, p. 423)

Although the amendment was not adopted, it still serves as evidence that the homeless were politically weak. When considered in light of the widespread and very vocal opposition to any mandatory AIDS testing policy, the fact that the homeless were targeted for the first federal legislation mandating AIDS testing is telling. This suggests that the amendment's sponsors thought that the homeless could not effectively retaliate against this intrusive and discriminatory policy (i.e., it seemed unlikely they could muster enough support to vote the policy's supporters out of office). Conversely, this exemplifies the type of policy directed at politically weak target populations.

Finally, as discussed earlier, the U.S. House of Representatives approved an amendment authorizing local communities to enforce "workfare" laws for the able-bodied homeless (Blakely, 1987, p. 423). Here too is evidence of the homeless target population's relative political weakness. Being required to work for assistance clearly suggests that the federal government is in the position to dictate terms to an undeserving target population, in this case the able-bodied homeless. Returning to the example of typical FEMA-aid recipients, natural disaster victims are not required to work for their disaster relief. And yet it is safe to assume that many in this target population are able-bodied.

THE MCKINNEY ACT'S SUB-TARGET POPULATIONS

In its division of the homeless into sub-target populations, the unamended version of the McKinney Act was consistent with then-contemporary knowledge and wisdom concerning homelessness. David A. Snow et al. (1986, p. 407) reported that discussion of homelessness prior to the passage of the McKinney Act centered on two issues: the number of homeless and the characteristics of the homeless.

As suggested earlier, there was also great controversy among scholars, journalists, and advocates concerning the characteristic make-up of those without homes. Again, much of this debate focused on questions of whether the appropriate social scientific method was employed and/or whether data were interpreted correctly (e.g., see Snow et al., 1986, 1988; Wright 1988). Nevertheless, some divisions within the homeless population were broadly acknowledged. For example, Thomas J. Main divided homeless shelter users into three broad sub-populations: "the mentally ill, the alcoholics and drug abusers, and the 'economic only' youths" (1983, p. 25). More specifically, many scholars (e.g., Bassuk, 1985; Lamb & Talbott, 1986; Levine & Stock-dell, 1986) reported that a sizable number of the homeless—ranging from roughly one-tenth to one-half of the total homeless population—were mentally ill. Similarly, numerous studies found that many homeless experienced alcoholism and other forms of drug addiction, for example, a National Institute of Mental Health demonstration project found that roughly 40 percent of homeless were alcoholics and 15 percent were drug abusers (reported in Whitman, 1990, pp. 36–37; cf. HUD 1989). Other accounts (Kozol, 1988) suggested that homeless people and the poor in general were ill-trained and in some cases, illiterate. There were also numerous, although vehemently contested (e.g., see Whitman, 1990; Kondratas, 1990), reports concerning the growing number of intact families within the overall homeless population (Foley in Committee on Banking, 1987, p. 30; Kozol, 1987; Whittemore, 1990). In addition, attention was being focused on the growing number of homeless women with children (Bassuk, 1985; 1986). Still, other reports that children were the fastest growing subgroup of the homeless were gaining currency around this time (Cuomo in Committee on Banking, 1987, p. 36; Rivlin, 1986; Kozol, 1987). Yet other commentators (Marin, 1987; Wright & Lam, 1987; Marcuse, 1988) identified the combination of individual economic hardship and an insufficient supply of low-cost housing as an important cause of homelessness.

The McKinney Act reflects many of these same divisions in the way it describes homeless individuals and in the programs it establishes and funds on their behalf. It specifically refers to the following sub-target populations: Adults, At-risk Persons, Children, The Elderly, Families, The Handicapped, Homeless Individuals, Low Income People, The Medically Underserved, The Mentally Ill, Migrant and Seasonal Workers, Native Americans, Substance Abusers, and Veterans. Upon a close reading of the McKinney Act, it is apparent that age, family status, physical and mental fitness, one's ability to read, and one's status as a Veteran and/or as a Native American are the bases for subdividing the overall homeless target population.

Consider the following examples. The McKinney Act's preamble reads: "To provide urgently needed assistance to protect and improve the lives and safety of the homeless, with special emphasis on elderly persons, handicapped persons, and families with children" (101STAT.482). Similarly, subtitle A—Primary Services and Substance Abuse Services—of title VI suggests that some homeless are alcoholics and/or drug addicts. Subtitle B—Community Mental Health Services—of the same title indicates that some homeless are mentally ill. In addition, subtitles A—Adult Education for the Homeless—and B—Education for Homeless Children and Youth—of title VII suggests that at least some of the homeless lack education and/or are illiterate, and that some of the homeless are children.

Rationales for the division of the homeless into these subgroups typically centered around the claim that there is no one set explanation for homelessness. People become homeless for a variety of reasons, some simple, some complex. The McKinney Act itself offers the following rationales for these divisions:

> the causes of homelessness are many and complex, and homeless individuals have diverse needs; . . . there is no single, simple solution to the problem of homelessness because of the different subpopulations of the homeless, the different causes of and reasons for homelessness, and the different needs of homeless individuals. (101STAT.484)

Sub-Target Populations Missing from the McKinney Act

The authors of the McKinney Act avoided using gender, sexuality and ethnicity—with the exception of Native Americans—as bases for subdividing the overall homeless target population. This is worth noting since homelessness poses different problems for men and women, for persons with different ethnic backgrounds and racial characteristics, and for people of different sexual orientations. As examples, homeless men probably do not share the fear of rape that homeless women and homeless children do. Similarly, heterosexual homeless persons probably do not experience the fear of physical violence and rape that lesbian, gay, bisexual, and transgender homeless adults and teens experience. While privacy and personal security are serious issues for all homeless persons, it should be clear that homeless women and children, and lesbian, gay, bisexual, and transgender homeless persons have even greater needs for protection and privacy than do some other homeless persons.

This is also worthy of note because, as suggested earlier, many advocates for the homeless conscientiously worked to sway public sentiment toward helping the homeless. Much of this work involved using the media and academic presses to challenge "traditional" homeless stereotypes. Academicians and advocates argued that the homeless included working families, women with children, women without children, people of color discriminated against by the dominant culture, etc. For example, homeless women—as victims of spousal abuse, as mothers of children, etc.—were repeatedly discussed in the academy (e.g., see Hunter et al., 1991; Council on Scientific Affairs, 1989). In the popular press, accounts of "bag ladies"–not bag men—were repeatedly presented to the public. Yet the McKinney Act does not specifically address the unique needs of women without homes.

In contrast, some sub-target populations originally absent from the McKinney Act (e.g., persons with AIDS) were recognized in later authorizations and/or in companion legislation. As only one additional example, the rural homeless do not appear in the original act. It was not until the 1992 reauthorization (Public Law 102–550) that the needs of the rural homeless were directly addressed by federal lawmakers through HUD's Rural Homelessness Grant program (106STAT.4035). However, the invisibility of homeless people in rural areas appears consistent with the absence of wide-spread discussion of their plight in the media and in the academy (cf. Goodfellow, 1999; Goodfellow & Parish, 2000). Writing in 1991, Zawisza explained:

> Few studies address the extent of homelessness in rural or nonmetropolitan areas. Those that do tend to focus on people who receive shelter or other types of assistance. . . . Studies that provide some useful estimates suggest that 5 to 14 percent of the nation's homeless population is in nonmetropolitan areas. (reprinted in Roleff, 1996, p. 55)

Indeed, Laudan Y. Aron and Janet M. Fitchen noted, "It is only in recent years that the presence of homeless people in rural American has been widely acknowledged" (1996:81). This is reflected in the late addition of federally funded programs specifically addressing the problems experienced by the rural homeless.

CRITICAL ANALYSIS

Looking back over this chapter, three points meriting greater attention stand out.[9] First, in a perverse way, portraying various subgroups of homeless in public debate, in the press, and in the McKinney Act, deflected attention from structural causes and systemic factors that facilitate homelessness.

While the McKinney Act's subdivision of the homeless into subgroups may have enabled the creation of some effective policies designed to meet the needs of individual groups of the homeless in a time of crisis, it has also perpetuated a stopgap approach to homelessness. For example, attention to the homeless with mental health problems or substance abuse problems was deemed necessary to secure additional mental health and/or substance abuse treatment programs (cf. Baum & Burnes, 1993, p. 28). Recognition of the growing number of homeless families not only proved a good tactic for winning public sympathy for the homeless, but it has also facilitated the creation of programs directed at the special needs of families; as only one example, Arizona's Maricopa County created a school specifically for homeless children (see Willey, 1994).

Similarly, the acknowledgment that many homeless women and children come from abusive households strengthened activists' calls for the creation of domestic violence shelters for battered women and children. Identification of homeless veterans as a sizable sub-population allowed for the VA to better provide services to these needy veterans. Similarly, the identification of homeless Native Americans has allowed for the creation of programs designed to address their specific needs.

But the classification of the homeless into one or more of these subgroups focuses attention on the problems and failings of individual homeless or the character faults of groups of homeless. Homeless mentally ill people are individuals who possess individual mental health problems that can be blamed for their homeless condition. The substance abuse problems of many individual homeless people can be used to explain their homelessness. The aberrant behavior of abusive spouses and/or parents is to blame for the homeless state of many women and children. Similarly, post traumatic stress syndrome may be offered as an explanation for the homelessness of many individual veterans. And some may invoke racist characterizations and stereotypes to account for homeless Native Americans.

Notice that in each of these scenarios, the economic and political policies underpinning homelessness are easily missed. For example, many commentators pointed out that the extraordinary increase in mentally ill homeless persons occurred as a direct result of the nation's deinstitutionalization policies in the 1960s and 1970s.[10] Still, no coherent policy addressing this systemic problem has been enacted. This may be partially explained because our contemporary economic structure sustains this situation. To seriously respond to our society's earlier decision to no longer institutionalize great numbers of mentally ill persons in psychiatric hospitals would entail a substantial modification of the U.S. health care system and a corresponding alteration of the economic system. Such reforms run counter to those with vested interests in the current system. Moreover, there are political costs for those politicians who would raise the ire of big business and other well-funded special interests. Recall the political cost to former First Lady Hillary Rodham Clinton in her efforts to promote a national health care insurance program. The National Hospital Association very shrewdly employed a well-funded advertising campaign centered on a fictitious couple, Harry and Louise, to ferment popular opposition to this initiative. As a result of this campaign, Hillary Rodham Clinton was forced to take a less visible political role in national affairs for the remainder of the Clinton presidency.

As another example, recognition of the plight of homeless Native Americans—and of the obviously unjust conditions that exist on reservations in general—has not resulted in reforms (or even serious proposals) that address the inherent economic and political inadequacies of the reservation system. Again, to adequately address these issues might require that federal and state governments reallocate economic resources to the reservations and perhaps even renegotiate, in good faith this time, the sovereign status of Native American peoples. This is certainly against the interests of many. Just think of the political ruckus raised in those state legislatures across the country where gaming is allowed on reservations.

In terms of Marx's methodological approach discussed earlier, this piece-meal approach to homelessness facilitates a stopgap response that does not address the larger structural arrangements fostering contemporary homelessness. Missing in the McKinney Act and related legislation is a systemic response to the underlying structural causes of much contemporary homelessness. While the individual problems facing various subgroups of homeless are identified and partially addressed in the McKinney Act, lawmakers never adequately reintegrate or synthesize these insights into a coherent whole that allows an adequate response to homelessness.

Second, participants in the debate over homelessness that raged throughout the 1980s and into the 1990s typically presented arguments that were consistent with one of three general views of homelessness. These positions differ in terms of two variables: (a) whether or not individual homeless are considered responsible for their predicament; and (b) whether or not the government is held responsible for helping the indigent. I present these three general positions in a two-by-two format in Table 3.3. Admittedly, these are overgeneralized positions, but they do suggest how debate participants viewed and/or portrayed the "collective" homeless, the homeless in general, or the stereotypical homeless.

Table 3.3: (Over)Generalized Views of Individual and Federal Responsibility Toward the "Collective" Homeless

		Individual Responsibility of the Homeless	
		Yes	No
Government Responsibility for the Welfare of the Homeless	Yes	"Reformers" in favor of federal aid to the "collective" homeless; view the homeless as "Misguided"	"Liberals" in favor of federal aid to the "collective" homeless; view the homeless as "Victims"
	No	"Conservatives" opposed to federal aid to the "Collective" Homeless; view the homeless as "Deviants"	

Accordingly, many proponents of aid to the homeless argued that a large number of homeless individuals, if not most, are not personally responsible for their situation. Instead, such advocates argued that much of contemporary homelessness is driven by social, cultural, and economic forces beyond the control of homeless individuals. Accordingly, they argued that it is the federal government's responsibility to provide for their needs. I label such proponents "Liberals" in the table and throughout the remainder of this work. Such advocates of federal aid typically portray and speak of the homeless as "victims."

Other advocates of federal aid to the homeless suggested that most individual homeless are ignorant, unskilled or de-skilled due to changes in the economy and/or they are not mentally or physically able to adequately provide for themselves. Such advocates argued that society has a responsibility to reform, rehabilitate, and/or to educate homeless individuals so that they may overcome their individual failings and get out of their predicament. I label such advocates "Educators" in the table and in the remainder of this work. These proponents of federal aid typically portray and speak of the homeless as "misguided."

Opponents of federal aid to the homeless usually argued that while some homeless are deserving since they have physical or mental impairments preventing them from working, most homeless are undeserving. They are undeserving because they are willful agents who choose to be homeless rather than to work for their living. From this perspective, the appropriate response to homelessness is to make life for the willful, and thus undeserving, homeless more difficult and perhaps even to criminalize those aspects of their behavior that are offensive. Through employment of this strategy, the homeless should be given sufficient incentive to choose to find work and get off the public dole. I label those who espouse such views "Conservatives" in the table and in the remainder of this work. Such opponents to federal aid typically present and speak of the homeless as "deviants."

In forwarding one or more of these three perspectives in arguments concerning the McKinney Act, debate participants made use of a preexisting stock of cultural images concerning homeless in our society. For example, Conservatives seem to have approached the issue with a preconceived set of homeless characterizations in mind. This set can be traced to historical portrayals of homeless persons in various poems, literary and academic books, and statutes. As suggested earlier, these characterizations were almost always negative (e.g., derelicts, bums, vagrants, panhandlers, etc.). Not only did these characterizations appear to shape opponents' political posture toward the homeless, but they also served as prejudicial standards that the contemporary homeless had to overcome. Evidence of the strength of this wide-spread set of characterizations can be seen in the editorial column discussed above. The column was predicated on the belief that people are familiar with the homeless character types presented. Royko appears to assume that his description of "the Weeper" as a big-time "moocher" will elicit a fairly uniform image.[11] Further evidence of the strength of these characterizations can be found in the way that advocates for the homeless actively worked to counter these characterizations. In particular, they repeatedly discussed the various subgroup of homeless and appeared to downplay the existence and numbers of homeless who could readily be characterized as "derelicts" or "bums."

Furthermore, no matter which of the three perspectives was advanced, debate participants were greatly concerned with the moral justification of acting or not acting to assist the homeless. In fact, Conservatives, like the successful opponents of welfare who advocated its end, strategically focused attention on the work status of the homeless in order to suggest that the homeless are not morally deserving of aid.

Opponents of the McKinney Act typically argued that because the homeless did not work, they did not deserve assistance or sympathy. Review of the debate over homelessness presented in this chapter indicates the importance of one's work status for determining moral deservingness. This is further evidenced by the fact that advocates for the homeless do not contest this belief. In fact, many advocates for the homeless—and critics of recent welfare program revisions as well—also see work as an important part of the solution to homeless. As only one example, Reverend Conway testified during the U.S. House subcommittee hearing on Urgent Relief for the Homeless Act discussed earlier:

> Just one final note. That is about unemployment. Most of the homeless who use our transitional shelters need jobs. They need them not only to be able to afford housing, but more fundamentally, because the dignity of human life depends on work. In justice, all these able-bodied people have a right to employment and decent wages. (reprinted in Committee on Banking, 1987, p. 80)

Accordingly, I present a detailed discussion of the role that work plays in shaping consideration of homelessness in the next chapter. I do so by offering an abbreviated presentation of the historical appearance of each of the three general positions on homelessness identified here. Similarly, given the role that historically grounded portrayals and characterizations played in the creation of the McKinney Act, I also call attention to how those we now consider to be homeless were characterized in the past next chapter.

Third, a sense of science seems to permeate discussion of homelessness. Some of those engaged in this debate couched their arguments in scientific terms. Indeed, some Liberals, some Educators, and some Conservatives employed the mantle of science to bolster their political arguments, regardless of whether or not their positions were supported by sound scientific research. For example, many participants in this debate presented their arguments so that they appeared to be based on objective truths derived from natural and scientific laws. This is evidence that science carries a positive normative valuation in our society and that it plays an important rhetorical function. As an example, recall Reverend Conway's testimony before the U.S. House of Representatives subcommittee on the Urgent Relief for the Homeless Act presented earlier. He pointed out that there is no "real understanding of the problem" of homelessness and bemoans the fact that only one scientific study of questionable merit has been conducted on homelessness in the Chicago area (appearing in Committee on Banking, 1987, p. 79). His decision to respond to this single scientific study suggests the weight that even one scientific study carries.

Similarly, many other debate participants focused their attention on methodological issues and questions of the scientific efficacy of various studies. For example, much of the debate between Liberals, Educators, and Conservatives revolved around questions concerning what groups constitute the homeless, how many homeless exist and which estimate of the number of homeless is most accurate, which homeless are mentally ill and/or substance abusers, and what is the most effective way to address the special needs of such homeless. As hinted at in the previous sections, science as a narrative with connotations of universal and objective laws and science as an ideograph plays an important role in delimiting consideration of homelessness and social welfare in general. Therefore, in chapter 5 I present a critical review of science and its role in these matters.

Chapter Four
"Homelessness" in Context

... in speaking of poverty, let us never forget that there is a distinction between this and pauperism. The former is unavoidable evil, to which many are brought from necessity, and in the wise and gracious Providence of God. It is the result, not of our faults, but of our misfortunes. They, who are thus poor, claim our tenderest commiseration, our most liberal relief; they are our brethren and our sisters . . . Pauperism is the consequence of wilful error, of shameful indolence, of vicious habits. It is a misery of human creation, the pernicious work of man [sic], the lamentable consequence of bad principles and morals . . . Relief to the poor is charity: but the relief of pauperism, though in many cases perhaps unavoidable, and where refusal would be apparently inhumane, seems to generate the evil in a tenfold degree (Charles Burroughs, delivered on the occasion of the opening of the New Almshouse in Portsmouth, N.H., December 15, 1834; reprinted in Burroughs, 1971, pp. 9–10).

Men [sic] make their own history, but they do not make it just as they please; they do not make it under circumstances chosen by themselves, but under circumstances directly found, given and transmitted from the past. The tradition of all the dead generations weighs like a nightmare on the brain of the living. (Karl Marx in Marx & Engels, 1978, p. 103)

As suggested in the previous chapter, the terms of debate surrounding the McKinney Act over the issue of homelessness were usually limited to one of three general views about the homeless. However, when discussion of homelessness is carefully analyzed, we find that some opponents and advocates of federal aid to the homeless made arguments grounded in more than one of these three views. Furthermore, at times the tone of the debate and the moral indignation that some debate participants expressed suggest that more was at stake than merely the allocation of federal money for homeless relief.

Given the voracity of this debate, I suggest that these three positions correspond to different ideologies, or perhaps more accurately, to different regimes of truth as discussed in chapter 1. As particular regimes of truth, each of these general views about the homeless developed in particular historical contexts and became the basis for public laws and policies at particular times. Therefore, not all of these views have coexisted and affected public policy at all times as they do today. For example, I argue that the regime of truth corresponding to today's Liberal position is relatively new. Its development and expansion roughly parallels the origin and increased usage of the term "homelessness." In fact, this term was used repeatedly by advocates for the homeless as they worked to recast the homeless in more favorable terms.

Homelessness refers to the state of being without a home, and as such it suggests a condition of passivity or being on the part of the homeless rather than of activity or doing. According to the second edition of the Oxford English Dictionary (OED), the term "homelessness" came into use in the nineteenth century, the OED reports that it appears in a Dickens work from 1848 (OED 1989). However, the OED reports that the term "homeless" has been in use since at least 1615.

Still, the term "homeless" does not carry the negative baggage that some other terms used to describe people without homes do. Apparently many of these terms have been in use longer than the term "homeless," and certainly in circulation much longer than the term "homelessness." For example, the OED reports that the term "beggar" has been in use since at least 1225; "vagabond" since at least 1426; "vagrant" since at least 1444; "pauper" since at least 1493; "sturdy beggar" since at least 1538; "rogue" since at least 1570; and "tramp" since at least 1664. In comparison to homelessness, some of these terms connote greater activity and hence, a greater sense of agency. For example, vagabond signifies one without a home who wanders or roams from place to place. The verb form of vagabond, vagabonding, has been in use since at least 1586, while the term describing the state of being associated with vagabonds, vagabondage, has only been in use since the nineteenth century (1813), according to the OED. Similarly, consider the term "tramp." While it has been used as a noun since at least the seventeenth century, the term signifying the condition of being a tramp, trampage, has only been in use since the nineteenth century (1894). Still, the verb tramp, meaning to tread or walk with a firm step, has been in use since at least the fourteenth century (1388).

I suggest that these terms developed in response to, and reflect, different and shifting social relations and cultural values. Therefore, they roughly correspond to different regimes of truth. For example, homelessness suggests a state of being that corresponds to the Liberal stance. Accordingly, just as the term homelessness did not exist prior to the middle of the nineteenth century, I argue that before the nineteenth century the Liberal stance was not conceivable as a viable social or political view the way it is today (cf. Dean, 1991, p. 28).

Nevertheless, when examined collectively, the Liberal, Educator, and Conservative positions reflect the West's changing attitude toward individual and governmental responsibility (cf. Dreyfus & Rabinow, 1982, p. 144). Detailed knowledge of these shifts and of the rise of competing perspectives concerning indigence, should better enable the homeless and their supporters to counter claims that "things have always been this way" or "that's just the way things are."

Accordingly, the next three sections of this chapter entail readings of each of these regimes of truth as they are reflected in the development and underlying assumptions of public policy concerning indigence.[1] This is premised on the idea that particular perspectives or regimes of truth concerning the homeless are enshrined in public policies. In presenting my analysis of public policies and related texts, I call attention to the way that the different positions forwarded in contemporary arguments over the homeless draw upon the images, portrayals, social constructions, and assumptions underlying these regimes of truth. Thus, I suggest that echoes of each of these regimes of truth could be heard reverberating in debate on the McKinney Act; indeed, they can still be heard echoing in contemporary debate on homelessness. In this way I describe the manner in which public policies and social constructions mutually influence one another. Furthermore, I call attention to the shifting role that work has played in justifying particular stances and policies toward the destitute in general. This has been particularly important in recent discussion of homelessness since work and morality appear so intertwined.

Therefore, in the following sections I illustrate the rise and spread of the regime of truth underlying today's Conservative stance through a reading of the development of early English vagrancy laws. I present the rise and spread of the regime of truth underlying today's Educator stance through an analysis of the development and institutionalization of Alms-houses in the U.S. And finally, while the predominance of the regime of truth underlying the Liberal stance seems questionable given retrenchments in social welfare programs over the last decade, this position clearly has been influential. Evidence of its importance can be found in the wording of the McKinney Act. Therefore, I highlight the rise of this regime of truth through discussion of the development of New Deal social welfare legislation. However, England's vagrancy laws did not develop in a vacuum. They were promulgated within preexisting legal, political, and social systems. Therefore, in the next section of this chapter, I briefly examine the general context in which these laws developed.

But before beginning my analysis, let me briefly discuss three potential dangers inherent in approaching the development of regimes of truth or dominant ideologies as I do. First, as discussed in chapter 1, discussion of ideologies may seem to suggest that there is a discoverable truth masked by the ideology. However, I do not support this view, and it is for this reason that I prefer to use the phrase "regime of truth" instead of ideology in my analysis.

Second, discussion of predominant ideologies or regimes of truth and my presentation of each of the three particular regimes of truth in separate sections may appear to suggest that these views were all-pervasive at one time. But this was not the case. Although the views of personal and governmental responsibility I present in each of the following sections may have been more widely held and/or articulated than other views in a given historical era, they were not the only views. There were clearly competing views affecting laws, policies, social practices and social institutions. My presentation partially reflects this in the way the sections overlap one another.

Third, by presenting the development of these three regimes of truth in chronological order, it may seem that I am suggesting that these historical events led inevitably to the present as we experience it. In essence, my examination of the development of three regimes of truth in different historical epochs may appear to suggest that today's "understanding" of the homeless necessarily followed from the preceding events. However, this is not my argument. As discussed above, my analysis suggests how views concerning the homeless, as presented in the McKinney Act and related debate, were possible. It does not follow that it must necessarily have developed as it did because of historical events or the existence of predominant ideologies or regimes of truth.

PRE-VAGRANCY LAW VIEWS

England's vagrancy laws were created to address specific problems that developed within an extant social, political and legal context. In this sense, the regime of truth reflected in the English Vagrancy laws developed within a preexisting regime of truth. For example, seventy-five years prior to the passage of the first vagrancy laws, Edward the first promulgated the following edict in 1274:

> Because the Abbeys and houses of religion have been overcharged and
> sore grieved, by the resort of great men and other, so that their goods

have not been sufficient for themselves, whereby they have been greatly hindered and impoverished, that they cannot maintain themselves, nor such charity as they have been accustomed to do; it is provided, that none shall come to eat or lodge in any house of religion, or any other's foundation than of his own, at the costs of the house, unless he be required by the governor of the house before his coming hither (3 Edw., c. 1; reprinted in Chambliss, 1964, p. 68)[2]

Ten years later, Edward I passed the following ordinance for Wales:

. . . that the Westours [Welsh for unbidden guest], Bards, Rhymers, and other idlers and vagabonds, who live upon the gifts called Cymmortha [Welsh for aid, assistance or help],be not sanctioned or supported in the country, lest by their invectives and lies they lead the people to mischief and burden the common people with their impositions (No. V. Ex. Record Carnarv., fol 81; reprinted in Ripton-Turner, 1887, p. 35).

These statutes offer at least two noteworthy insights into thirteenth century England and Wales that help to contextualize the later vagrancy statutes. First, apparently it was normal and even expected that religious institutions and individual households indiscriminately provide charity to those who sought it. C. J. Ripton-Turner reports that "among the vices of that rude age parsimony was rarely one, the exercise of charity being in fact regarded as a religious duty" (1887, p. 61). He presents the poem *Stimulatus Conscientia* or *Prick of Conscience,* penned in 1349 by Richard Rolle, a hermit in the St. Augustine order and a doctor of divinity, to bolster his observation (reprinted in Ripton-Turner 1887, p. 44).

When thou mayst help through wisdom and skill,

And will not help, but holdest thee still

That some good ask at thy door,

Be it without, be it within

Yet it is a venial sin

Sidney Webb and Beatrice Webb write: "Throughout all Christendom the responsibility for the relief of destitution was, in the Middle Ages, assumed and accepted, individually and collectively, by the Church. To give alms to all who were in need . . . were duties incumbent on every Christian . . ." (1927, p. 1; see also Kelso, 1922). Similarly, A. L. Beier explains, "During the High Middle Ages there was a tendency to idealize poverty. St. Francis, for instance, taught that beggars were holy, and that the holy should live as beggars" (1985, p. 4). In fact, the need to prohibit the provision of aid suggests that charitable giving was a widespread and frequently practiced social custom at the time (cf. Ripton-Turner 1887, p. 44).

Therefore, following the dissemination of this custom, negative moral judgments probably were not tied to the receipt of charity as they often are today. This also suggests that questions concerning the personal responsibility of individual needy persons were not typically considered once this social custom gained wide currency.

However, Brian Tierney points out that even in the twelfth and thirteenth centuries, people were capable of distinguishing between "holy poverty and idle parasitism," and he cites the last testimony of St. Francis to support his claim: "'I have worked with my hands and I choose to work, and I firmly wish that all my brothers should work at some honorable trade. And if they do not know how, let them learn . . . '" (reprinted in Tierney, 1959, p. 11). Still, Tierney argues that "while . . . idleness was condemned and poverty was not automatically equated with virtue, there was no disposition to go to the opposite extreme and assume that a state of destitution was necessarily indicative of moral turpitude" (1959, pp. 11–12). In addition, some argue that charitable giving was considered an indication of one's moral integrity (e.g., Jones, 1969; Webb & Webb, 1927). Still, it is noteworthy that between the two edicts Edward promulgated, both alms-receiving and alms-giving are legally restricted.

There are at least two possible rationales for the creation of these measures. First, on the surface, it appears that many people who were not truly in need of charity were taking advantage of this custom, hence the need to restrict this practice. Second, perhaps these measures were motivated by the desire to stop the provision of aid to all, regardless of whether they were truly needy or not. As the Welsh ordinance suggests, by the late thirteenth century, there was concern that the idlers and vagabonds who took advantage of charitable giving might lead the commoners astray. This suggests that the idle life of the entertainer and vagabond was considered mischievous by the legal authorities. Accordingly, the recipients of charitable aid are socially constructed as mischievous and burdensome in the edict. Through this edict the terms beggar and idler take on a derogatory connotation. This is accomplished through the association of the terms idler, beggar, mischief and burden.

Second, the desire for social order seems to be the rationale behind the second measure. The first measure was designed to provide financial relief to religious institutions through the legal restriction of alms-receiving, and the second was designed to prevent future mischief through the legal restriction of alms-giving. While the provision and receipt of charitable aid were legally restricted through these measures, no substitute measures designed to provide aid for the needy were offered. Clearly, neither edict offers any hint that the monarchy had any obligation to aid the needy. This suggests that aiding the indigent was not considered a necessary function of the monarchy in this era. Instead, apparently maintaining the status quo or social order was the monarchy's primary responsibility (see Tierney, 1959).

Therefore, as evidenced by these attempts to legislate new values concerning charitable giving and the receipt of such aid, the regime of truth from which the English vagrancy laws developed did not hold individual people responsible for their indigent condition. Perhaps questions of individual responsibility were considered irrelevant in the earlier regime of truth. Furthermore, the fact that the monarchy only enacted legislation designed to provide for the most rudimentary needs of its people—security from crime and relief from the burdens of charity—indicates that the monarchy was not considered responsible for the care of the indigent.

Table 4.1: (Over)Generalized Views of Individual and State Responsibility Toward the "Collective" Indigent Before the First Vagrancy Laws

		Individual Responsibility of the Homeless	
		Yes	No
Government Responsibility for the Welfare of the Homeless	Yes		
	No		"Virtuous Christians" charity is an individual and/or church responsibility; view the "collective" indigent as **"The Meek"**

Considered in light of the two-by-two table presented at the close of the previous chapter, the regime of truth that 3 Edw., c. 1 and No. V. Ex. Record Carnarv., fol 81 attempted to alter fills the bottom right cell. Proponents of this earlier view might be labeled "Virtuous Christians," given the historical context (see Table 4.1). Indigent and homeless people might have been presented as "God's Poor" or "the Meek" by those holding these beliefs.

If a particular regime of truth or dominant ideology was grounded in these views, we would expect to find traces or echoes of these views in contemporary discussion of homelessness (cf. Gramsci, 1971). In fact, some contemporary arguments regarding homeless and indigent people do reflect these beliefs. For example, arguments for the federal government to get out of the business of poor relief completely so that religious charities, private philanthropists and good corporate citizens, and more recently, compassionate conservatives, may provide poor relief unencumbered by bureaucratic interference seem to recall the Virtuous Christian stance. However, such arguments were not made as frequently in debate over the McKinney Act as arguments reflecting the other three positions described in chapter 3, or for that matter, as frequently as they have been made since the 1990s. Similarly, the idealization of poverty discussed earlier can be heard faintly reverberating in contemporary society as well. For example, it echoes in the pejorative description of contemporary Western society as "Babylon" by some homeless youth and by some members of the rainbow family (see Niman, 1997; cf. Amster, 1999).

ENGLISH VAGRANCY LAWS THROUGH THE REVOLUTION

England's first vagrancy law, entitled Statutum de Servientibus (Statute of Laborers), was prepared in 1349 by King Edward III's court.[3] The ordinance made it illegal for anyone to give alms to any unemployed person of sound mind and body. Its reads:

> Because a great part of the people, and especially of workmen and servants, late died of the pestilence, many seeing the necessity of masters and great scarcity of servants, will not serve unless they receive excessive wages, and some rather willing to beg in idleness than by labour to get their living; We, considering the grievous incommodities which of the lack especially of ploughmen and such labourers may hereafter come, have . . . ordained:

> That every man and woman . . . able in body, and within the age of threescore years, not living in merchandise, nor exercising any craft nor having of his own whereon to live, nor proper land, about whose

tillage he may himself occupy, and not serving any other, if he in con-
venient service (his estate considered) be required to serve, shall be
bounded to serve him which shall him require . . . And if any such man
or woman, being so required to serve, will not the same do . . . he shall
anon . . . committed to the next gaol, there to remain under straight
keeping, till he find surety to serve in the form aforesaid.

That if a workman or servant depart from service before the time
agreed upon, he shall be imprisoned.

That the old wages and no more shall be given to servants.

That if the lord of a town or manor do offend against this statute in
any point, he shall forfeit the treble value.

That if any artificer or workman take more wages than were wont to
be paid, he shall be committed to the gaol.

That victuals shall be sold at reasonable prices.

Item, because that many valiant [able-bodied] beggars, as long as they
may live of begging, do refuse to labour, giving themselves to idleness
and vice, and sometimes to theft and other abominations; it is
ordained, that none, upon the said pain of imprisonment shall, under
the colour of pity or alms, give anything to such, which may labour, or
presume to favour them towards their desires; so that thereby they
may be compelled to labour for their necessary living.

That he that taketh more wages than is accustomably given, shall pay
the surplusage to the town where he dwelleth, towards a payment to
the King of a tenth and fifteenth granted to him. (reprinted in Ripton-
Turner, 1887, pp. 43–44)

In 1350 the ordinance was amended so that freemen—former serfs or
slaves and their descendants who, after manumission, enjoy due Process of
Law—were no longer allowed to seek summer employment wherever they
desired. "An none shall go out of the town where he dwelled in winter, to
serve the summer, if he may serve in the same town" (25 Edw. III., stat. 1;
reprinted in Chambliss, 1964, p. 68).

Leaving aside debate over the "true" motivation of these early
vagrancy laws (see Slack, 1995; cf. Beier, 1985; Chambliss, 1964; 1989;
Adler, 1989), it is possible to identify some of their rationales, intended target populations, and likely consequences. At face value, the vagrancy ordinances were created in an attempt to restore social order or the status quo

in the aftermath of the plague and to prevent potential shortfalls in the production of commodities. Authorities attempted to accomplish these goals by mandating a reduction in the price of labor and by forcing itinerant servants and freemen to return to work. It is noteworthy that penalties were established for the idle and for those giving aid to the idle, as well as for those paying servants more than the "old wages."

The vagrancy law and its first amendment specifically target four different groups. In doing so, the laws present each target population in a different light. Owners of manorial estates appear in a positive light since they were the direct recipients of benefits in the form of the legally dictated labor of servants, freemen, and beggars for a reduced wage. Clearly the freedom of the owners of manorial estates was impinged to a much lesser extent than that of their servants, freemen, and beggars. Only the owners' freedom to give alms was restricted while the others' personal freedom was greatly restricted. In fact, the prohibition against giving alms actually may have been a benefit for the owners of manorial estates; that is, if the owners were giving alms only because of moral pressure, then these measures gave them a legitimate rationale to stop giving alms.

Persons engaged in merchandise and trade appear in a more neutral light since they were exempt from the heavy burdens that servants, beggars, and freemen experienced. Still, they were not provided with the same direct benefits that the owners of manorial estates were provided. However, it seems that they may have benefited by a more stable social order; e.g., a reduction in the number of thefts.

Beggars are presented in a negative manner and were assigned significant direct burdens in the form of forced employment for set wages and a restriction of their personal freedom to seek other employment or remain idle. Similarly, those freemen laborers who usually engaged in seasonal work were also the recipients of burdens in the form of a limitation of their freedom to seek better employment in other locals.

At least four points merit attention before considering later vagrancy legislation. First, compared with the 1274 statute, this statute emphasizes the willfulness of beggars and the idle. This statute implies that individuals are personally responsible for their fate by repeatedly drawing attention to choices that the idle and beggars make, some willingly beg rather than work, and some willingly refuse to serve needy masters. Second, like the Welsh ordinance discussed earlier (No. V. Ex. Record Carnarv., fol 81), this statute presents begging in association with idleness, vice, and mischief. But in this statute, begging appears to be a cause of idleness, vice, and sometimes of theft and other abominations. Therefore, beggars and the idle poor are presented in a negative light. They are socially constructed as greedy, short-sighted, and selfish, and even as criminals. They are greedy because many will work only for excessive wages. They are short-sighted and selfish since they do not take into account the hardships their willful (in)activity may cause in the future, and they are criminals because many engage in criminal activities. Third, according to the preamble, the monarchy is moved to act to restore social order and to prevent future social disorder in the form of a reduction in commodities production. Fourth, like the thirteenth-century measures discussed above, this ordinance makes no provision for poor relief. In fact, there is still no hint that the monarchy has any responsibility to provide aid to the indigent.

As the context and circumstances that facilitated the development of the vagrancy laws changed, their emphasis and stated purposes changed as well. Paul Slack explains: "The first Tudor poor laws of 1495 and 1531 were largely concerned with ways of punishing vagrants and sending them home, though the second added that deserving paupers could be licensed to beg" (1995:9). In particular, the preamble of the 1531 statute entitled "How Aged Poor and Impotent Persons compelled to live by alms shall be ordered" reads:

> where in all places throughout this Realme of Englande, Vacabundes and Beggers have of longe tyme increased & dayly do increase in great & excessyve nombres by the occasyon of ydelnes, mother & rote of all vyces, wherby hath insurged & spronge & dayly insurgethe & spryngeth contynuall theftes murders & other haynous offences & great enormytes to the high displeasure of God . . . & damage of the Kyngis People & to the marvaylous disturbance of the Comon Weale of this Realme. . . . (22 Hen. VIII., c. 12; reprinted in Ripton-Turner, 1887, p. 73)

The statute reads in part:

> If any person, being whole and mighty in body, and able to labour, be taken in begging, or be vagrant and can give no reckoning how he lawfully gets his living; . . . and all other idle persons going about, some of them using divers and subtle crafty and unlawful games and plays, and some of them feigning themselves to have knowledge of . . . crafty sciences . . . shall be punished as provided (reprinted in Chambliss, 1964, p. 71).

Chambliss reports that the statute also distinguishes between different types of vagrant offenders; it mentions a specific concern with categories of "unlawful" behavior, and it applies a punishment typically reserved for serious criminals—cutting off an ear (1964, p. 72). The statute also decreed that alms were to be given to a common box (community chest) rather than to beggars directly, and it made provisions for justices to fine those giving aid to able-bodied vagrants (Leonard, 1900, pp. 55–56).

However, unlike the earlier laws, this statute acknowledges that there is need for poor relief in some cases. As Walter I. Trattner explains:

> The act . . . contained constructive features concerning relief of the poor; it decreed that . . . local officials 'shall make diligent search and inquiry of all aged poor and impotent persons which live or of necessity be compelled to live by alms of the charity of the people,' and assign such people areas where they may beg. (1974, p. 8)

Still, this statute seems to be much more concerned with defining and addressing criminality than with providing poor relief. In fact, Webb and Webb write that "there is no evidence that this [statute] made any provision for the destitute" (1927, p. 45). In comparison to the earlier vagrancy laws, this statute is more narrowly focused on criminality (see Chambliss, 1964; Trattner, 1974). For example, whereas the fourteenth-century laws targeted groups in a variety of social classes, including the owners of manorial estates, persons engaged in merchandise and trade, and freemen and beggars, the 1531 statute directly targeted only some in the poor social class—beggars, vagrants, vagabonds—in the name of the abstract group, "King's People." Here again the connection between idleness and criminal behavior is made clear. Indeed, idleness is presented as the origin (mother and root) of all vices ultimately leading to thefts, murders, and other offenses. Therefore, this statute furthers the 1351 measure's social construction of beggars and the idle as mischievous criminals.

Like the earlier vagrancy statute, the rationale offered to justify this measure was concern for the internal security of the realm and the need to restore social order. Similarly, this statute offers no evidence that the monarchy had a responsibility to provide aid directly to the indigent. While a division is made between old and impotent persons who were to be allowed to beg legally in designated areas and the able-bodied idle who were to be severely punished, central authorities still had no apparent responsibility to provide poor relief to anyone.

However, it is worth noting that even as the monarchy was furthering the criminalization of idleness, it was also taking steps to address some of the causes of unemployment and vagrancy. In 1514 and 1515, two separate acts prohibiting the destruction of houses and the conversion of farmland into pastures were promulgated (see Nicholls, 1854, p. 111). In 1533–34, 25 Hen. VIII., c. 13 was passed. Its purpose was to prevent additional farm consolidation and the further conversion of farmland into pasturage for wool production. The statute attributes the criminal behavior of some of the poor to increased prices for staple goods. Its preamble suggests that this increase results from reduced production in favor of increased wool production. The act reads in part: "By reason whereof a marvellous multitude of the people . . . be not able to provide meat, drink, and clothes for themselves, their wives, and children, but be so discouraged with misery and poverty that they fall daily to theft, robbery . . . or pitifully die for hunger and cold" (reprinted in Nicholls, 1854, p. 112). Here then is evidence of not only a concern with the causes of vagrancy, but also an administrative attempt to address one cause. This suggests the existence of an alternative outlook concerning poverty and vagrancy at this time. Yet even here, these three measures do not suggest that the monarchy has a responsibility to provide aid directly to the impoverished.

However, historians do not appear to view these measures as key to the development of English poor laws. For example, Ripton-Turner (1887) does not even discuss the 1514 and 1515 acts in his history of vagrancy. Similarly, in his work entitled *The English Poor Law, 1531–1782,* Slack does not consider the 1533–34 act, 25 Hen. VIII., c. 13, to be one of the more important statutes relating to the poor (see Slack, 1990, p. 51). E. M. Leonard omits all three of these statutes from his analysis, *The Early History of English Poor Relief* (1900), and Kelso also omits all three measures in his discussion of the English roots of poor relief in Massachusetts (1922). Rather, all four authors highlight the punitive statutes in their histories of English poor laws. This seems to suggest that the authors of these works viewed these three measures as exceptions to the rule vis-à-vis the dominant views in the sixteenth century. In fact, the perspective underpinning these measures was not acted upon systematically again until the nineteenth century in England and in the United States (cf. Webb & Webb, 1927, p. 79).

Therefore, as illustrated in the 1349 (2 Rich. II., stat. 1, c. 8), 1350 (25 Edw. III., stat. 1) and 1531 (22 Hen. VIII., c.12) measures to criminalize idleness and mandate labor discussed previously, we see evidence of the changing view of personal responsibility. In comparison to the view of the indigent as the meek, or as God's poor, these laws present the indigent as willful criminals who are responsible for their fate. After all, the 1531 statute states that these criminals commit acts against God and the realm. Indeed, Beier suggests that in the fifteenth, sixteenth, and seventeenth centuries, the terms beggar, vagabond and rogue may have carried the derogatory connotation and rhetorical impact that terms such as anarchists, communists and terrorists do today (1985, p. 6). Therefore, they could not be the victims of fate or merely the subjects of God's will. From this perspective, vagrants are considered willful agents. Accordingly, they are presented as responsible for their idleness and other vices.

Conversely, the criminalization of vagrancy (idleness) presents labor and work in a positive or moral light. Since vagrancy is a crime against the Realm and God and hence immoral, vagrants are not only criminals, they must also be immoral. But what makes vagrancy a crime? Idleness or the absence of work. Here then absence of work is equated with negative qualities. Considered through the lens of differentiation discussed in chapter 1, the term from which the original is distinguished often takes on the opposite valuation. In this case, since non-work is presented as immoral, then its opposite, work, may appear moral in comparison.

Still, the 1349, 1350 and 1531 laws do not offer evidence of a change of view concerning the monarchy's role. The monarchy's responsibility still appears tied to security, peace, and order. However, it does not appear to be obliged to provide the indigent with direct aid.

Accordingly, I argue that these laws reflect a different regime of truth. Considered in light of the two-by-two table discussed earlier, this regime of truth fills the bottom left cell. Those who accept this regime of truth might be labeled "Keepers of Order," given the overt concern with

Table 4.2: (Over)Generalized Views of Individual and State Responsibility Toward the "Collective" Indigent Implicit in Early Vagrancy and Poor Laws

		Individual Responsibility of the Homeless	
		Yes	No
Government Responsibility for the Welfare of the Homeless	Yes		
	No	**"Keepers of Order"** government's responsibility is to maintain social order; view the "collective" indigent as **"Criminals"**	**"Virtuous Christians"** charity is an individual and/or church responsibility; view the "collective" indigent as **"The Meek"**

maintaining social order expressed in these laws (see Table 4.2). Indigent and homeless people might be labeled "the idle," "vagabonds," "beggars," "criminals," and a little later as "rogues" by those holding this perspective.

Like the regime of truth corresponding to the Virtuous Christian stance, the regime of truth unpinning the Keeper of Order perspective also underscores some recent arguments concerning homeless persons. In fact, arguments drawing upon the imagery and assumptions of the Keeper of Order stance are commonplace today. For example, recall U.S. Representative Quillen's comments presented at the start of chapter 3. He argued: "I don't want the Congress to create more homelessness on our streets. Instead of solving the problem, we would make it entirely more complicated" (reprinted in Blakely, 1987, p. 422). Also, since the passage of the McKinney Act, many local governments have passed "get tough" ordinances directed against homeless and indigent persons (see Conner, 1993; Mac Donald, 1994; Smith, 1996; Foscarinis, 1996b; Amster, 1999). Such measures include the prohibition of camping in urban parks and public spaces, restrictions on panhandling and restrictions on congregating on public lands. But more than that, some local governments have passed measures designed to inhibit if not actually prohibit the provision of assistance to homeless individuals. As examples, Winter (2003) reports that "in San Francisco from 1993 to 1995, police arrested more than 700 people for feeding the poor without a permit, in violation of a city ordinance;" that "in 2000, the United Methodist Church in Portland, Oregon was ordered by city officials to shut down a meals program for the homeless it had been running for 16 years. The program, the church was informed, violated 'smart growth' laws;" and that "in 2003, Santa Monica, California passed an ordinance that limited feeding programs for the hungry on the grounds they attracted unwanted homeless people."

In arguing for such measures, Conservatives often employ rhetoric paralleling that of the Keepers of Order to describe homeless people; recall the rhetorical descriptions of the homeless as "drinking, doping, loitering, panhandling, defecating, urinating, molesting, stealing" made during the city council meeting in Santa Barbara, California, presented in the previous chapter. In this rhetoric, the homeless are presented as vile criminals. Similarly, the Not In My Back Yard (NIMBY) phenomenon has been, and continues to be, a strong force that advocates for the homeless and policy makers must overcome to provide services for homeless persons. Often the proponents of NIMBY present the homeless in terms that harkens back to the rhetoric of early vagrancy statutes. For example, at a public meeting called to discuss the opening of a day center for homeless men in a London neighborhood, a local resident testified:

I have been beaten up a number of times by these people. . . . I have lived and worked here for 12 years. I work in my shop 12 hours a day and there are people here who want to put a centre for these men next door to me. They come into my shop when their social security money has gone and they beg food of me. They accost young people in the streets. They strip in front of me, they have sex on the green, they couldn't care less where they have sex. That's the kind of people you want to put next to me. (reprinted in Cook & Braithwaite, 1979, p. 4)

The 1531 poor law (22 Hen. VIII., c. 12) was rescinded in 1536 and replaced with a new statute bearing the same name. While the new statute continued most of the 1351 statute's measures, including the punishment of beggars and the idle, it also filled in the gaps left by the previous statute (Ripton-Turner 1887, p. 81). In particular, it addressed issues concerning the provision of aid to impotent and aged poor persons. The statute ordered that local church officials:

> shall take such discreet and convenient order, by gathering and procuring voluntary alms of the good Christian people within the same, with boxes, every Sunday and holiday, or otherwise among themselves, in such good and discreet wise as the poor, impotent, sick, and diseased people, being not able to work, may be provided, holpen, and relieved; and that such as be lusty, having their limbs strong enough to labour, may be daily kept in continual labour, whereby every one of them may get their own living with their own hands. (27 Hen. VIII., c. 25; reprinted in Nicholls, 1854, pp. 121–122)

It further stipulated how the charitable giving was to be encouraged. It prohibited direct alms-giving to the poor. It required parish officials to maintain records of charitable collections and the distribution of poor relief, and it set penalties for anyone found embezzling poor relief funds. It further decreed that surplus funds collected in richer parishes should be distributed to poorer parishes (Eden, 1757, pp. 83–87). And, in a step that furthered the conflation of idleness and begging with crime and immorality, it also made vagrancy a capital offense in some situations.

In 1563, the statute was reinforced with the passage of another measure (5 Eliz., c.3). Like the earlier measures, this one also clearly distinguished between the impotent and able-bodied poor. However, unlike the earlier measures, it added a compulsory element designed to provide needed funds for poor relief. It authorized bishops to require those who were unwilling to contribute voluntary alms to appear before the local justices of the peace during their regularly scheduled sessions. In turn, local justices were instructed to politely urge and persuade the uncooperative to contribute alms voluntarily. If justices were unable to do this, they were authorized to impose a tax upon the uncooperative for poor relief.

These last two measures have special significance for the later development of poor relief in the United Kingdom and the United States. These statutes are the first to claim that the State (central government) has a responsibility to directly aid the poor—a claim often made by contemporary activists who advocate federal relief for homeless persons—and to explicitly legislate nation-wide governmental measures for this purpose. In reference to the latter statute, Webb and Webb write, "Here . . . we have, in germ, the legally compulsory and universally payable Poor Rate" (1927, p. 52) and Nicholls notes that "[t]his is the first instance of a compulsory assessment for the relief of the poor" (1854, p. 152).

These measures are not only important for this reason but also for the way they direct secular government to intercede on behalf of the indigent. The administration of relief was to be handled at the local level primarily by ecclesiastical officials at the parish level, justices of the peace, and municipal authorities, not through a centralized administrative unit overseen directly by the central government. In this way, these measures served as precedents affirming the primacy of local government over State government in matters of poverty and homelessness, even though it is the central government that promulgated the laws. This is noteworthy since lawmakers were certainly aware of alternative approaches to poor relief. Slack writes: "Poverty might have been dealt with by scores of workhouses and almshouses, as it was in the Low Countries, or by major institutions, general hospitals of the kind erected in French cities and even begun in London. All these existed in England" (1995, p. 9).[4]

In 1572, these earlier innovations were codified in a statute entitled "An Acte for the Punishement of Vacabonds, and for Relief of the Poore & Impotent" (14 Eliz., c. 5). However, as suggested in its title, its primary concern was with punishing the idle poor (Chambliss, 1964, p. 73). In addition, the statute furthered the trend to classify vagrants into different types noted in the statute of 1531. In fact, the statute differentiated between ten different classes of rogues and vagrants (see Ripton-Turner, 1887, pp. 107–108). In so doing, it furthered the conflation of poverty and criminality. The statute also set new fines for any who harbored or gave money and/or lodging to vagrants or rogues.

This was followed by a number of other statutes that built upon and strengthened these trends. Noteworthy are the 1598 statutes (39 Eliz., c.3 & c.4) that repealed all previous vagrancy statutes. The 1598 statutes synthesized many of the earlier measures by redefining rogues and vagabonds, setting new punishments for those defined as such, and requiring them to return to their place of birth or last residence. The latter measure also authorized the employment of civil administrators to implement the policy. As Webb and Webb explain, "The . . . statute for the first time puts in the forefront the civil power, by requiring the appointment, in every parish, of Overseers of the Poor, and by specifically imposing on them, in conjunction with the Church-wardens, the duty of providing for all the various classes of the destitute" (1927, p. 64). Still, it should be noted that the civil administrators were to be chosen by local officials, not appointed directly by officials of the State.

This legislation was reenacted in 1601 (43 Eliz., c.2.) in what some point to as the beginning of the old poor law (cf. Leonard, 1900, p. 133; Trattner, 1974, p. 10). In the years leading up to the English Civil War (1642–1646), other versions of the 1601 statute were enacted, and minor amendments were passed. However, some suggest that these later statutes—in fact, all of those passed between 1590 and 1640 concerning indigence—are not as important individually as they are collectively since they reflect a trend toward greater centralized authority. Webb and Webb describe these measures as an attempt by the Privy Council to establish an "administrative hierarchy" (1927, p. 60; see also Dean, 1991, p. 21). But they argue that this movement was interrupted by the English Civil War:

> After the Restoration there was no resumption of the hierarchical national administration. 'This elaborate system . . . depended on the cooperation of central and local authorities; the Civil War gave it a shock from which it could not recover. The machinery which had lain [sic] to the hand of Elizabeth's advisers for the regulation of social and industrial conditions was no longer available.' (Webb & Webb 1927:99; quotation from Cunningham, 1903, p. 203)

Still, Slack argues that: "the collapse of Charles I's personal rule in 1640, which ended central direction for good, did not therefore lead to the collapse of social policy, as was once thought. Justices were no less active after 1640 in the tasks they had learnt since 1598: quite the contrary" (1995, p. 15; cf. Webb & Webb, 1927, p. 78). Instead, poor relief became an almost exclusively local concern once again. As Mitchell Dean explains:

> One of the legacies of the revolutionary period was to loosen the governance of the Poor from the 'administrative hierarchy' and to place it within the framework of the local social and political order . . . Poor relief was administered on a mostly local basis for the next century and a half in the tiny administrative unit of the parish by officials elected by ratepayers assembled in 'vestries.' (1991, p. 24)

As suggested earlier, these latter measures and the popular opposition to central authority reflected in the English Civil War played an important role in the development of U.S. public policy addressing indigence. Recall that the Mayflower brought the first Puritan pilgrims to Massachusetts in 1620.[5]

THE INSTITUTIONALIZATION OF ALMS-HOUSES IN THE U.S.

While the movement toward a centralized, "administrative hierarchy" directing poor relief policy failed to take hold in the colonies and U.S. during the seventeenth or eighteenth centuries, other English legal approaches to poverty and perspectives on indigence did take hold. Many of the legal approaches to poor relief and views of the poor underpinning the Elizabethan Poor Law of 1601 (43 Eliz., c.2) and earlier laws served as guides for colonial policies (Cray, Jr., 1988, p. 36; Chambliss, 1964, p. 75).

For example, "Rhode Island merely stated that the basis of its poor law would be 43 Elizabeth . . ." (Katz, 1996, p. 14). As more specific examples, Pennsylvania's first poor law entitled "An act for the relief of the poor" (1705), closely followed 39 Eliz., c.3 & c.4 and 43 Eliz., c.2 by establishing overseers of the poor at the township level throughout the colony. It also empowered the overseers to assess and collect a tax for the provision of poor relief (Philadelphia Board of Guardians of the Poor, 1971, pp. 3–7).

Pennsylvania's second poor law, "An act for Supplying Some defects in the law for the relief of the poor" promulgated in 1718, also parallels 39 Eliz., c.3 & c.4 and 43 Eliz., c.2 in the way that it required that any non-resident of a community likely to become a burden to that community be forcibly returned to the place from which he or she came. It also stipulated that recipients of poor relief were to wear an identifying letter (a large Roman P) on their clothing, and it restricted aid to only the impotent poor (Philadelphia Board of Guardians of the Poor 1971, pp. 8–13). Furthermore, it repeated the earlier laws' concern with social order and their negative portrayal of the idle. It reads in part: "And to the end, that the monies raised only for the relief of such as are impotent and poor may not be misapplied and consumed by the idle, sturdy and disorderly beggars" (Philadelphia Board of Guardians of the Poor, 1971, p. 11).

Similarly, a supplemental Pennsylvania act passed in 1734 begins:

> WHERE AS it is found by experience, that the laws of this province made for the relief of the poor, and for removing and punishing rogues, vagrants, and other idle and disorderly persons, wandering about the country, have not proved effectual for the good purposes for which

they were intended, and for securing the inhabitants of this province from being oppressed with great charges, arising by such idle and disorderly persons, coming from the neighbouring colonies. . . . (Philadelphia Board of Guardians of the Poor, 1971, p. 13)

These three Pennsylvania acts parallel a number of the earlier English statutes and ordinances in that they sought to discriminate between the deserving poor and the undeserving idle. In fact, according to many commentators of the day, such discrimination was a moral necessity. As only one example, in a sermon delivered August 12, 1752, Charles Chauncy preached:

Indulged habitual Idleness is a Reproach to any Man, whether he be high or low, rich or poor. We were made for Business. Both our Souls and Bodies are so constituted, as Exercise is a great and necessary Means to keep them in an healthful and vigorous State . . . Industrious Labour is therefore the Law of *Christianity*. Instead of altering this Method appointed by God . . . for the Support of Life, the Gospel has confirmed it. . . . And to support Man in Sloth, tho' they should disguise their Guilt under the Cover of the most pios Pretences, is a virtual setting up our own Wisdom in opposition to the Wisdom of God, and subverting the Method he established, both in *the nature of Things,* and by *positive Revelation* . . ." (Chauncy, 1971, pp. 7 & 11).

Indeed, Chauncy could be no more explicit when he declared: "Whenever Persons are *idle,* they are *disorderly:* For an idle Life is, in the whole of it, a *Disorder*" (1971, p. 13). Indeed, according to the preamble, the first three Pennsylvania poor laws were justified not only by desire to provide relief for the truly needy, but also by the need to maintain social order through the punishment of vagrants, rogues, and the idle.

Many of these colonial policies and perspectives continue to shape contemporary debate and policy on homelessness in the U.S. In particular, the English colonies and the eventual United States inherited at least four guiding principles from the English experience with poor relief. First, central government has a responsibility to maintain social order. Second, secular government has a responsibility—albeit a limited one—to provide for the welfare of the deserving poor. Therefore, it is necessary to distinguish between the deserving and undeserving poor. Third, work is a continuing concern affecting poor and vagrancy policies. On the one hand, poor relief should be limited to the impotent poor who cannot work. On the other hand, the able-bodied poor should be punished and forced to work. Fourth, poor relief is first and foremost a local affair (cf. Katz, 1996, p. 14). Clearly, some of these principles underlie the Keeper of Order view discussed earlier; by extension, some of these principles presage today's Conservative perspective.

Still, today's social and political landscapes entertain other principles and perspectives. Specifically, other general views of government responsibility and personal culpability play a crucial role in framing contemporary debate and policy options concerning homelessness. Therefore, it is noteworthy that some of these inherited principles appear to contradict the Conservative perspective. In fact, some of these principles correspond to a fundamentally different view—a view underpinning what I label the Educators perspective.

However, through most of the nineteenth century—arguably up to the 1930s—a powerful, active, centralized national government was considered an affront to local and state autonomy and something to be resisted. Accordingly, poor relief was not addressed by the federal government. Therefore, the Reformer view is not enshrined in national laws and policies. Instead, I suggest that it roughly corresponds to the institutionalization of alms-houses in the nineteenth century.[6]

Throughout the eighteenth and nineteenth centuries, various policies concerning pauperism and vagrancy were implemented by local and state governments, by private charitable societies, and by church-affiliated charities. Nevertheless, by 1850, publicly and privately supported institutions founded specifically to care for the mentally ill, rehabilitate juvenile delinquents and provide for the destitute had become the predominant means of addressing these issues (Katz, 1996, p. 11; see also Cray, Jr., 1988, p. 101). In the case of the indigent, the alms-house was the most commonplace institution employed.

However, as discussed earlier, alms-houses did not originate in the nineteenth century. In Europe, alms-houses were used in the Low Countries and in London in the sixteenth century. In the English colonies, a number of larger towns and cities built alms-houses: Boston, Massachusetts, in 1664; Salem, Massachusetts, in 1719; Portsmouth, New Hampshire, in 1716; Newport, Rhode Island, in 1723, Philadelphia, Pennsylvania, in 1732, New York City, New York, in 1736, Charleston, South Carolina, in 1736, Providence, Rhode Island, in 1753; and Baltimore, Maryland, in 1773 (reported in Katz, 1996, p. 15). These earlier experiences are significant because they were offered as evidence to support the construction of alms-houses in various municipalities across the country (e.g., see Burroughs, 1971, p. 22).

Alms-houses were often expected to accomplish conflicting goals, and because of this, they experienced numerous problems. Consider the following excepts from an 1827 report commissioned by the Board of Guardians of the Poor of the City and Districts of Philadelphia:

The great defect of our Alms House is, that from want of room, adequate accommodations for the employment of the paupers cannot be had; and from its imperfect construction, a suitable classification of the inmates cannot be effected. That the aged and infirm, who have never forfeited their title to respect, and are the victims of disease and misfortune, should be indiscriminately mingled with the brutalized victims of excess and crime, is a state of things that ought not to be tolerated. It is subjecting those already too much east down, to a new degradation, and is a further unmerited addition of misery and oppression. 'On the other hand, if the vicious are permitted to enjoy the comforts, and partake of the indulgences, which are due to age and misfortune alone, their condition becomes not only supportable, but eligible. The fear of poverty is diminished and the shame of dependence is obliterated. Public establishments become thronged, as will never fail to be the case, whenever Alms House support is better than or even equal in its kind, to the support to be obtained by labor.' (Philadelphia Board of Governors, 1971, p. 25)

The report continues:

> The poor in consequence of vice, constitute here and everywhere, by far the greater part of the poor. The experience of every Institution your committee visited is decisive on this point. From three-fourths to nine-tenths of the paupers in all parts of country, may attribute their degradation to the vice of intemperance. . . . 'Indolence, intemperance, and sensuality . . . are the great causes of pauperism in this country.' (Philadelphia Board of Governors, 1971, p. 26)

The report's authors further proclaim that:

> . . . it is the great duty of every society to take care, that their Alms Houses should be provided with space and accommodations, to enable those who have the superintendence of them, to provide work for this class, and for every class in it, according to its ability; to the end, *that they should never become the resort of idleness, for indulgence; nor of vice for comfort; nor of disease for cure, without cost.* (Philadelphia Board of Governors, 1971, p. 27)

This report presents a number of themes and assumptions concerning the indigent, four of which warrant greater attention. First, advocates of almshouses apparently assumed that it is appropriate to discriminate between the deserving and undeserving indigent. This view is supported by numerous other sources. For example, recall Charles Burroughs' comments concerning the clear distinction between poverty and pauperism presented at the start of this chapter. As another example, consider the speech entitled "An Address on Pauperism, Its Extent, Causes, and the Best Means of Prevention." R. C. Waterson prepared and delivered the speech to the Society for the Prevention of Pauperism on February 4, 1844. In it he proclaimed that there were three classes of poor: "First—Those who are supported from day to day by their honest industry . . . Second—Those who are willing to work, but from old age and feebleness, or disease, are not able, by their labor, to meet their necessary expenses . . . Third—Those who might work, but who *prefer* IDLENESS; who have no self-respect or desire to be useful" (Waterson, 1971, p. 5). Note that in each of these examples, the apparent appropriateness of discriminating between the classes of poor reinforces the Keeper of Order view that individuals are personally responsible for their actions.

Second, although advocates of alms-houses argued that the truly needy indigent should be separated from the undeserving poor and provided with needed aid, this was not typically practiced. In fact, miserable living conditions in the alms-house were to serve as a disincentive for the idle and able-bodied poor to seek aid. So, even though the authors of the Philadelphia Board of Governors' report presented above expressed regret for the way that the deserving indigent were forced to live with the undeserving poor, they also admitted that the wretched conditions reinforce "the fear of poverty" and "the shame of dependence." Looking back at Massachusetts' early alms-houses, Kelso wrote: "They admitted of slight if any separation of the sexes. They afforded no classification according to age. They housed little children with the prostitute, the vagrant, the drunkard, the idiot, and the maniac" (1922, pp. 112–113). In this way, in spite of ideals to the contrary, the actual practices of alms-houses furthered the association of poverty with criminality, idleness, and insanity—associations that often reappear in many contemporary social constructions of the homeless. Indeed, writing in 1822, Josiah Quincy argued:

> Among all the general relations of man, the most interesting to the individual, and the most important to society, are those of poverty, vice, and crime. They are, in truth, often little else than modifications of each other; and, though the class of virtuous poor form an honorable exception to the fact, yet in the more depressed classes, they are so frequently found together, that in every general survey, they may be

considered, for the purpose of analysis and remark, in some measure
as inseparable. (1971a, p. 3)

As another example of the poor conditions that characterized many
alms-houses, Katz reports extraordinary mortality rates at the Erie
County Poorhouse: in 1848, 1 out of every 6 alms-house resident died; in
1849, 1 out of every 8 died; and in 1854, 1 out of every 9.16 died (1983,
p. 65). Conditions appear to have been so bad that in 1856, the editor of
the *Buffalo Medical Journal* was moved to write: "The whole policy of
the Poorhouse is niggardly and mean. Cheap provisions, cheap doctors,
cheap nurses, cheap medicines, cheapness everywhere is the rule, forget-
ting the higher policy which finds true economy in a humane policy"
(reprinted in Katz, 1983, p. 66).

Third, requiring the recipients of poor relief to work was a great
focus of concern. In fact, the Philadelphia alms-house's failure to provide
work for its residents was viewed as its "great defect" by the report's
authors. But beyond requiring work for its own sake, advocates of alms-
houses typically expected work to serve two distinct purposes. Mandatory work was supposed to lead to the inculcation of work habits, and to
help offset the cost of providing poor relief. As an illustration of these
concerns, in 1819 the alms-house of Salem, Massachusetts, reported that
it is "always a principal object with the Overseers to give as much of an
active character to the employments of the poor, as the age, strength, and
general habits of the persons to be employed will admit" (reprinted in
Quincy, 1971b, p. 29). Similarly, in 1818, the administrators of the alms-
house of Pepperbell explained: "Thus we infer, that as it relates to this
town, and we see nothing why it will not apply to other towns, the
method of supporting the poor in Poor Houses, is most advantageous,
attended with the least expense and most conducive to habits of temper-
ance, industry and economy" (reprinted in Quincy, 1971b, p. 35). As a
final example, even in arguing for the abolition of public poor relief,
Joseph Tuckerman admitted:

> But it still may be a noble charity to found a workhouse, which, while
> it gives support, and requires compensation for it from him who shall
> receive it, at the same time confers, with the support so given, the
> unspeakable greater good of that moral instruction and disciplined
> which shall call forth new and better dispositions than were ever
> before possessed, and do what can be done for the formation and
> establishment of a better character. (1874, p. 176)

From these passages, it is clear that the institutionalization of alms-houses was predicated on the belief that work and earning one's keep is good, moral, and virtuous. Conversely, idleness and begging were considered bad, immoral, and vile.

The pervasiveness of these beliefs is evidenced in the writings of some of the poor themselves. As an example, in 1893, hobo William Aspin confided: "Now I want you to distinctly understand me. I am not a Bum. I'd rather be kicked than go up to a House and ask for something to eat. I have went hungry many a time almost starved before I would ask. I often wished I was more of a Bum when I was good and hungry" (reprinted in Bruns, 1980, p. 100). Or consider the oath taken by members of the fraternal order of hoboes under the auspices of Hoboes of America, Inc. (1908).

> I . . . do hereby solemnly swear to do all in my power to aid and assist all those willing to aid and assist themselves. I pledge to assist all runaway kids, and to try to induce them to return to their homes and parents. I solemnly swear never to serve as a scab or a strikebreaker against any labor organization, and do all in my power for the betterment of myself, my organization, and organized labor, so help me God (reprinted in Bruns, 1980, p. 118).

Similar views frequently appear in contemporary debate on welfare and homeless aid.

Still, even though depictions of this type were prevalent, they were not uncontested (see Katz, 1989, p. 3). For example, the following passage appeared in the July, 1828, edition of the *London Quarterly Review.*

> Posterity will scarcely credit the extent to which the popular feeling has been worked upon, and warped, *by the ravings of our modern economists.* They, truly, have done all that in them lay, *to extinguish in the breasts of the more opulent classes, every spark of generous and benevolent feeling towards the destitute and needy pauper.* In their eyes, pauperism is a crime for which nothing short of absolute starvation can form an adequate punishment. (reprinted in Carey, 1971, p. 4)

Moreover, counter to portrayals of the indigent as lazy, shiftless, immoral, and vile, romantic constructions of vagabonds and hobos as rebellious free-spirits were offered and put into circulation by some of the poor themselves. Celebrated hobo Dan O'Brien describes the hobo:

He is the man in whom wanderlust is the strongest lust . . . reckless, perambulating soldier of fortune. . . . trifling things don't bother him. . . . He is an avowed optimist, laughs a great deal at the gyrations of men, looks upon politicians as tyrants, the clergy as supreme dodgers of things religious, hopes the human race, like whiskey, will improve with age. (c. 1920; reprinted in Bruns, 1980, pp. 7–8)

And Robert Service published the following poem in 1921 (reprinted in Bruns, 1980, p. 7).

Haunting, taunting, that is the spell of it;

Mocking, baulking, that is the hell of it;

But I'll shoulder my pack in the morning boys,

And I'm going because I must;

For it's so-long to all

When you answer the call

Of Wan-der lust.

Similarly romantic portrayals have been associated with more contemporary beatniks, hippies, punks, and members of the rainbow family. However, like the romantic portrayals of their contemporary counterparts, resistant social constructions of hoboes and vagabonds do not appear to have significantly altered the overall negative view of indigent persons.

Finally, it was hoped that alms-houses would reform or rehabilitate the idle and incorrigible. Although the desire to reform or rehabilitate the poor is implicit in the Board of Governors' report previously mentioned, other sources present this goal much more explicitly. For example, Josephine Shaw Lowell writes:

The best help of all is to help people help themselves. That is, that instead of receiving the means of living, men should receive from the benevolent the means of earning a living—that the poor man or woman should have the road cleared so that they may themselves march on to success—that their brains should be released from ignorance, their hands freed from the shackles of incompetence, their bodies saved from the pains of sickness, and their souls delivered from the bonds of sin. (1884, p. 96)

Similarly, in arguing for sweeping changes in the overall approach to poor relief, Waterson argues that "[m]uch Pauperism proceeds from Ignorance, and the remedy of this must of course be Education" (Waterson, 1971, p. 31). Katz claims that alms-houses were premised on the assumptions concerning the possibility of "reform, rehabilitation, and education." He writes that the sponsors of alms-houses "believed that institutions could improve society through their impact on individual personalities. . . . Even poorhouses shared in this rehabilitative vision; they would suppress intemperance, the primary cause of pauperism, and inculcate the habit of steady work" (Katz, 1996, p. 11). Therefore, although proponents and detractors of alms-houses disagreed on many points, both groups shared a concern with the causes of poverty and pauperism. In fact, much of the contention concerned the effectiveness of employing alms-houses to address the underlying causes of poverty. Proponents hoped that alms-houses would reform or rehabilitate the idle and incorrigible. Conversely, opponents argued that alms-houses actually exacerbated the problem and encouraged pauperism. (Compare the position expressed by the authors of the Philadelphia report above with the comments of Representative Clyde Holloway presented in chapter 3.)

Notice the subtle difference between the institutionalization of alms-houses as a policy and the earlier English vagrancy and poor laws. Except in the case of old, infirm, and impotent poor (only between 10 and 25 percent according to the authors of the Philadelphia Board of Governor's report) both approaches to poor relief hold the indigent accountable for their indigent conditions. However, unlike the Keeper of Order perspective which saw no need for direct government intervention on behalf of the indigent, the perspective underlying alms-houses *does* see a direct governmental role in the relief of the deserving poor and in the rehabilitation of those who are "poor in consequence of vice." Such poor were to be taught the value of work and thus to prefer work to idleness. They were to be educated on how to improve themselves so that they desire to be useful and thus gain a greater sense of self-respect, and they were to be weaned from alcohol.

Thus, eighteenth- and nineteenth-century concerns with the origins of extreme poverty and unacceptable behavior clearly differ from the fourteenth- and fifteenth-century vagrancy and poor laws discussed earlier. This difference suggests that the institutionalization of alms-houses across the U.S. represents another regime of truth. Those acting from within this regime of truth might be called "Reformers" since there is so much concern with rehabilitation and reform. From this perspective, homeless and indigent persons would be considered "drunkards," "idiots," "maniacs," and "prostitutes," but overall, they might be described as "misguided." In terms of the two-by-two table presented earlier, this regime of truth occupies the upper-left cell (see Table 4.3).

Table 4.3: (Over)Generalized Views of Individual and State Responsibility Toward the "Collective" Indigent Implicit in the Institutionalization of Alms-houses

		Individual Responsibility of the Homeless	
		Yes	No
Government Responsibility for the Welfare of the Homeless	Yes	**"Reformers"** government has a responsibility to aid deserving & rehabilitate the undeserving; view the "collective" indigent as **"Misguided"**	
	No	**"Keepers of Order"** government's responsibility is to maintain social order; view the "collective" indigent as **"Criminals"**	**"Virtuous Christians"** charity is an individual and/or church responsibility; view the "collective" indigent as **"The Meek"**

However, this is not a new perspective. Assumptions underpinning the 1514, 1515, and 1533–34 English measures discussed earlier were consistent with this perspective. In addition, premonitions of this regime of truth can be read in sixteenth-, seventeenth- and eighteenth-century humanist texts. Slack describes three key characteristics of early humanism: (1) Christian charity should serve rational ends besides furthering the donor's chances for salvation in the afterlife; (2) the rational end of Christian charity ought to be the moral reform of the poor; and (3) not only was social engineering possible, but it was a government responsibility (1995, pp. 6–7). As only one example, in the novel *Utopia* (1516), Thomas More's character Raphael Hythlodaye makes the following points during an exchange with a legally trained layman: "Simple theft is not so great a crime that it ought to cost a man his head, yet no punishment however severe can withhold a man from robbery when he has no other way to eat. In this matter . . . a good part of the world seems to imitate bad schoolmasters, who would rather whip their pupils than teach them" (1975, pp.

11–12) and "Yet this is not the only circumstance that makes thieving necessary. There is another one . . . Your sheep . . . that used to be so meek and
eat so little. Now they are becoming so greedy and wild that they devour
men themselves, as I hear. . . . For they leave no land free to plow: they
enclose every acre for pasture . . ." (1975, p. 14).[7] Clearly More's criticisms
are consistent with the nineteenth-century Reformer stance. However, his
concern for addressing the underlying causes of poverty and vagrancy were
not acted upon widely in the U.S. until alms-houses were institutionalized
during the nineteenth century.

Like the Virtuous Christian and Keeper of Order perspectives, the
Reformer stance can also be heard echoing in the rhetoric of some McK-
inney Act debate participants. As examples, recall Clyde Holloway's
comments presented earlier: "So my appeal to the Members would be to
vote no on this bill and send a message to the country that we are ready
to stand up and be heard. Let us go back to the work ethic in our country
that teaches us to work and earn our living" (1987, p. 1024). Reconsider
the comments of the program shelter director reprinted in chapter 3: "If
there was just someone to . . . sort of hit them over the head and say,
'hey, obviously this is not working . . . ' and really lead them through the
process, and teach them. . . . They are salvageable. They don't have to be
on welfare and they don't have to be homeless . . . (reprinted in Timmer,
1988, p. 164). Such arguments implicitly draw upon the regime of truth
underpinning the Reformer perspective. But not only does the Reformer
stance reappear in rhetoric concerning the homeless, it also affects contemporary public policy as well. On numerous occasions, the McKinney
Act directs aid recipients *not* to give cash aid directly to homeless persons. However, exceptions were allowed for " . . . nonprofit self-help
organizations established and managed by current and former recipients
of mental health services, or substance abuse services . . ."
(101STAT.514). Accordingly, cash payments could be given directly to
some groups of homeless persons if they are being reformed or rehabili-
tated according to society's standards.

NEW DEAL SOCIAL WELFARE LAWS

In comparison to the Virtuous Christian and Keeper of Order, and even the
Reformer perspectives, widespread belief in the appropriateness of an
active—not just reactive—central government taking responsibility for the
welfare of its indigent citizens is a recent development. Nevertheless, there
have been periodic calls for laws based upon this vision. For example, in

an 1824 report on poor relief produced by New York's Secretary of State, an anonymous letter-writer urges "that pauperism ought to be relieved in every instance at the expense of the whole community, each citizen bearing his [sic] equal proportion according to the value of his property, regardless of the locality or amount of pauperism in any particular spot where chance or circumstance might place it" (reprinted in Yates, 1971, p. 945). Writing in 1842, Walter Channing argues that, contrary to the popular view of poverty that looks for and finds its causes in the condition of indigence itself, "*a condition can never be a cause;* and a voluntary, a moral, an intellectual being, can hardly be the sole agent in the production of his own deepest misery" (1971, p. 21). He offers six propositions to help explain pauperism; among them: that social institutions and customs that separate people and produce distinct classes in the community produce and foster poverty (22); that the antagonism, opposition and drive for self-aggrandizement driving the patronage system of U.S. government produce and foster poverty (28); and that "the sudden reduction of wages, extended to large numbers, is not only directly injurious to wide interests, but produces pauperism" (35). Similarly, Edward T. Devine passionately sums up these views in his 1909 work, *Misery and Its Causes:*

> I hold that personal depravity is as foreign to any sound theory of the hardships of our modern poor as witchcraft or demoniacal possession; that these hardships are economic, social, transitional, measurable, manageable. Misery, as we say of tuberculosis is communicable, curable, and preventable. It lies not in the unalterable nature of things, but in our particular human institutions, our social arrangements, our tenements and streets and subways, our laws and courts and jails, our religion, our education, our philanthropy, our politics, our industry and our business (Devine, 1913, pp. 11–12)

He further argues that: "[w]e have no right to demand that the poor shall meet single-handed, as stray heroes have done, adverse conditions to which ordinary average human beings are not, as a matter of fact, ordinarily subjected" (Devine, 1913, p. 23). Notice that in these examples, the poor are socially constructed as victims of chance, adversity, and even as victims of structural arrangements and relations. In addition, these authors call for the government to alter social arrangements.

Still, there were far more calls for laws consistent with the Keeper of Order and Reformer stances than with this alternative vision. Such calls went unanswered by the federal government until the late 1800s. In fact, rationales reflecting these concerns only began to surface in federal policies in the latter part of the nineteenth century.

One of the earliest federal policies encapsulating this emerging perspective is the U.S. pension program for Civil War veterans established in 1862.[8] This view also underlies the federal government's establishment of a Children's Bureau in 1912. Similarly, a number of states implemented influential pension programs for mothers with children and for widows in the 1910s, 1920s, and 1930s that appear to reflect these principles (see Trattner, 1974; cf. Ward, 1997).

Debate leading up to the passage of the federal government's Smiths-Hughes Vocational Education Law in 1918 clearly offers evidence of the development of a new sensibility toward the poor and homeless. This act was for "'the promotion of vocational rehabilitation of persons disabled in industry or otherwise and their return to civil employment'" (reprinted in Cahn, 1924:672). Reuben D. Cahn writes that "[t]he traditional attitude toward cripples in the United States has been one of charity. We have regarded unfortunates with sympathy, but have considered their plight as one of inevitable helplessness and dependence" (1924, p. 665; see also Douglas, 1936). As suggested earlier, this charity has been provided usually by either private charities or by local governments. In fact, U.S. Speakers of the House Joseph Cannon and Champ Clark both opposed this measure because they viewed it as "paternalistic and visionary" (Cahn, 1924, p. 667). Still, as U.S. Congressman Mondell of Wyoming explained during floor debate on this measure, "Sentiment in favor of national leadership, stimulus, and direction in various lines in which the primary responsibility is local and in which the states and communities must wield the laboring oar . . ." was growing (reprinted in Cahn, 1924, p. 668).

However, the federal government did not pass and implement far-reaching, comprehensive social welfare policies until the mid-1930s. The New Deal marked the institutionalization of the welfare state in the United States. Passage of New Deal legislation became politically feasible because of the Great Depression (see Douglas, 1936). It was only with the failure of private charities, states, and local governments to adequately cope with the needs of the Great Depression's victims that President Franklin Delano Roosevelt (FDR) could act decisively. He directed the passage of the Federal Emergency Relief Act in 1933 (Public Law 73–30) over the protests of the entrenched business establishment and the prevailing political order. The act reads in part:

An Act To provide for cooperation by the Federal Government with the several States and Territories and the District of Columbia in relieving hardship and suffering caused by unemployment, and for other purposes.

Be it enacted . . . That the Congress hereby declares that the present economic depression has created a serious emergency, due to widespread unemployment and increasing inadequacy of State and local relief funds, resulting in the existing or threatened deprivation of a considerable number of families and individuals of the necessities of life, and making it imperative that the Federal Government cooperate more effectively with the several States and Territories and the District of Columbia in furnishing relief to their needy and distressed people.

SEC. 3. (a) There is hereby created a Federal Emergency Relief Administration . . . [it] shall cease to exist upon the expiration of two years after the date of enactment of this Act . . .

SEC. 4. (a) Out of the funds of the Reconstruction Finance Corporation made available by the Act, the Administrator is authorized to make grants to the several States to aid in meeting the costs of furnishing relief and work relief and in relieving the hardship and suffering caused by unemployment in the form of money, service, materials, and/or commodities to provide the necessities of life to persons in need as a result of the present emergency, and/or to their dependents, whether resident, transient, or homeless. (74STAT.55, 56, 57)

Two years later, on April 8, 1935, Congress passed a joint resolution entitled, "Emergency Relief Appropriation Act of 1935." It was designed "to provide relief, work relief and to increase employment by providing useful projects . . ." (Public Law 74–48). Among other things, this act established a number of public works programs to create jobs. Later that same year, FDR secured passage of the Social Security Act of 1935 (Public Law 74–351). This measure established major social insurance programs such as Social Security and Unemployment Compensation along with means-tested programs such as Aid to Families with Dependent Children and Supplemental Security Income. The act reads in part:

An Act To provide for the general welfare by establishing a system of Federal old-age benefits, and by enabling the several States to make more adequate provision for aged persons, blind persons, depended and crippled children, maternal and child welfare, public health, and the administration of their unemployment compensation laws; to establish a Social Security Board; to raise revenue; and for other purposes. SECTION 1. For the purpose of enabling each State to furnish

financial assistance, as far as practical under the conditions in such
State, to aged needy individuals. . . . (75STAT.620)

Note the difference between the rationales offered to justify these three measures and those offered to justify the English vagrancy laws and the development of alms-houses. Clearly the deprivation, hardship, and suffering of families caused by the Great Depression and the plight of the aged, blind, disabled children, and mothers were sufficient grounds to move the national government to intervene in local matters, to provide poor relief, and to create jobs for the unemployed.

But this was not the first time that dire economic conditions brought incredible suffering and deprivation to families and individuals. The suffering resulting from the enclosure of the commons in England in the fifteenth, sixteenth, and seventeenth centuries was probably just as dramatic, if not more so. Similarly, as capitalism developed and spread, it followed a repetitive boom and bust cycle (Mandel, 1978; Wallerstein, 1974; 1980; 1988). During the bust periods, depressions brought incredible hardships to many. For example, the depression of 1873 brought the U.S. economy to a standstill and great numbers of people lost their jobs, savings, and livelihoods (see Guedalla, 1936). However, none of these economic crises moved federal government authorities to relieve the suffering and hardship caused by unemployment as they did in the 1930s.

Therefore, I argue that the passage of the New Deal marks the embodiment of values based upon a distinct regime of truth. In terms of the two-by-two table presented earlier, this regime of truth fills the top right cell. Those embracing this regime of truth might be labeled "New Dealers." Holders of this perspective typically presented the homeless and other indigent persons as "the unemployed," "the needy," and "distressed victims of the depression." Generally, though, New Deal aid recipients were portrayed as "victims" of circumstances beyond their control. In contrast to the Keeper of Order and Reformer stances, the homeless and poor were not viewed as responsible for their indigent condition. New Dealers held that poverty and homelessness are driven by social, cultural, and economic forces. Accordingly, the federal government was expected to provide for the welfare of its needy citizens (see Table 4.4). But like the two preceding regimes of truth, the idea of work played a key role in the New Dealer perspective. Although New Dealers did not use work to differentiate between the deserving and undeserving poor, they did emphasize the creation of jobs as a means of redressing social ills and restoring a sense of personal worth and importance to the poor and homeless.

Table 4.4: (Over)Generalized Views of Individual and State Responsibility Toward the "Collective" Indigent Implicit in the Institutionalization of Alms-houses

		Individual Responsibility of the Homeless	
		Yes	No
Government Responsibility for the Welfare of the Homeless	**Yes**	**"Reformers"** government has a responsibility to aid deserving & rehabilitate the undeserving; view the "collective" indigent as **"Misguided"**	**"New Dealers"** federal government has an obligation to provide for the welfare of its needy citizens; view the "collective" indigent as **"Unfortunates"**
	No	**"Keepers of Order"** government's responsibility is to maintain social order; view the "collective" indigent as **"Criminals"**	**"Virtuous Christians"** charity is an individual and/or church responsibility; view the "collective" indigent as **"The Meek"**

As suggested earlier, it is debatable whether or not this view of government's role ever really took hold in the United States. Even in the face of economic disorder and political unrest brought about by the Great Depression, many raised strong objections to the intrusive nature of national programs and argued against any violation of state, local, and/or personal autonomy (see Piven and Cloward, 1971, pp. 82–83). For example, in rejecting pleas for the federal government to provide economic relief, President Herbert Hoover explained: "You cannot extend the mastery of government over the daily lives of the people without at the same time making it master of their souls and thoughts" (reprinted in Trattner, 1974, p. 231)—a view repeated by contemporary libertarian contributors to the debate on homelessness and welfare in general. Similarly, there was wide-spread negative sentiment concerning social welfare policies that were not tied to work. Such sentiment was commonplace even among recipients of direct poor relief. Donald Howard reports that respondents to an opinion poll taken in 1938 preferred work relief to the dole by a nine-to-one ratio (1943, p. 811). FDR himself appears to have been ambivalent—at best—about the desirability of permanent national social welfare policies (cf. Piven and Cloward, 1971). Indeed, Stoesz and Karger argue that FDR envisioned New Deal social welfare policies (except for Social Security) as only a temporary response to the Depression, designed to "salvage what remained of capitalism" (1992, p. 11). They argue that FDR intended to rescind most major New Deal programs once the crisis subsided.

Over time, and perhaps in spite of FDR's plans, national social welfare policies gained some sense of legitimacy. The federal government's growing role in addressing social ills appears to have gained some degree of acceptance as well. This can be explained partially because social welfare policies addressed serious, previously unmet needs. Similarly, the length, breadth, and gravity of the Great Depression left a strong impression on those who lived through it (cf. Sackton, 1997). For many of these survivors, social welfare policies are what prevented total disaster and ruin. By the 1950s, the idea of an expanding federal welfare state was neither alien nor completely antithetical to American values. Therefore, it should not be surprising that social welfare policies were expanded by the Kennedy and Johnson administrations through the Great Society and War on Poverty initiatives.

In fact, only very recently—perhaps as late as 1996 with the signing of the Personal Responsibility and Work Opportunity Reconciliation Act (Public Law 104–193)—has this perspective lost its sway over federal welfare legislation. For example, at the signing ceremony for the law, President Bill Clinton explained:

> Today, we are ending welfare as we know it. But I hope this day will be remembered not for what it ended, but for what it began—a new day that offers hope, honors responsibility, rewards work, and changes the terms of the debate so that no one in America ever feels again the need to criticize people who are on welfare, but instead feels the responsibility to reach out to men and women and children who are isolated, who need opportunity, and who are willing to assume responsibility, and give them to opportunity and the terms of responsibility. (1996)

Considered in conjunction with recent moves by local governments to criminalize behavior associated with the homeless and poor, these comments seem to indicate that public sentiment is now swinging away from the Liberals stances and toward the Educators and/or the Conservative approach.

DISCUSSION

The failure to oneself and one's family through paid labor is constructed in terms of three basic principles. First, productive work is an *individual* responsibility. With rare exceptions . . . blame for failure to find an adequate job is placed on the individual. Second, this failure is considered to be a *moral* one. Those who fail to work, without a socially approved excuse, at a socially approved job are condemned. They are defined as deviant. . . . Third, *moral degradation* of the poor is used as a negative symbol to reinforce the work ethic (Handler & Hasenfeld, 1991, p. 18; cf. Piven & Cloward, 1971).

This abbreviated story of the development of English vagrancy laws, the institutionalization of alms-houses, and the passage of New Deal legislation illustrates the context within which debate about the McKinney Act developed and the context within which contemporary discussion of homelessness is couched. In particular, my presentation of English vagrancy laws evidences what arguably came to be one of the dominant pre-modern and early modern stances toward homelessness and poverty—a stance that still affects consideration of homelessness. In oversimplified terms, to hold this stance is to view the homeless and poor as willful and responsible agents. From this perspective, the appropriate response to homelessness and poverty is to criminalize the aspects of this behavior that are offensive. Regardless of the cause of their predicament (be it God's will, the result of individual sins, or fate) the homeless and poor are to be dealt with as individuals and punished for violating social norms and laws.

My presentation of the institutionalization of alms-houses demonstrates what came to be the dominant stance toward homelessness and poverty in nineteenth-century America—a stance still heard reverberating in current arguments over homelessness. Simply put, to hold this stance is to consider the vast majority of homeless and poor to be willful and responsible agents who engage in inappropriate and even criminal behavior because they have been led astray or because they do not know any better. Therefore, government is held responsible for the rehabilitation of these lost souls.

My presentation of the passage of FDR's New Deal illustrates what came to be an important stance toward homelessness and poverty—a view that now appears to be waning. To hold this stance is to view the poor and homeless as victims of economic relations, social structures, and institutions. Accordingly, from this perspective, the appropriate response to poverty and homelessness is for the government to provide for the needs of the homeless and poor.

Looking back over the development of these different perspectives, at least four items are noteworthy. First, the rhetorical and legal context circumscribing debate on the McKinney Act was robust, complicated and even cluttered, just as contemporary debate about homelessness continues to be. Not only did three predominant positions on homelessness characterize that debate, but each of these positions drew from earlier stances reflecting different regimes of truth. This is depicted graphically in Figure 4.1. The social constructions, literary portrayals, characterizations and rationales corresponding to the Keeper of Order, Reformer, and New Dealer stances resonate in today's Conservative, Educators and Liberal stances. Accordingly, contemporary social constructions and characterizations of the homeless seem commonplace, and therefore, natural. This helps to explain how Representative Holloway could plausibly make his arguments concerning the homeless and how President Reagan could describe the homeless as "homeless by choice" without serious political fallout. They could do so because such claims politically served a significant part of their constituencies and because similar claims have been made repeatedly in our collective past. These claims appear to be based upon natural truths. This is important because this sense of familiarity, this sense

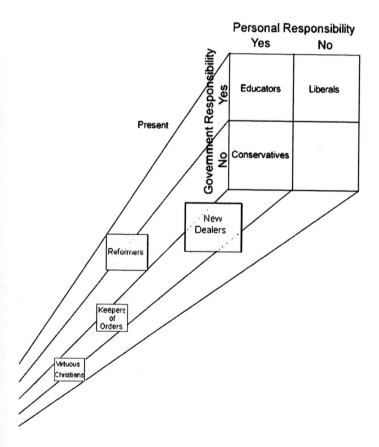

Figure 4.1: Perspectives on Poverty and Homelessness: Past and Present.

of timelessness, masks the contingent social arrangements underpinning homelessness and poverty, thus hampering those who opposed such portrayals and political policies premised on such portrayals. In other words, these earlier characterizations, portrayals and social constructions facilitate the reification of "the homeless" and "the poor," thus they partially hinder the political efforts of those who seek to address the structural underpinnings of poverty and homelessness.

Second, all four regimes of truth have not coexisted on equal terms historically. While some arguments made during debate over the McKinney Act do appear to be grounded in the Virtuous Christian stance, these arguments were relatively rare—even mute—in comparison to the numerous arguments based upon the other three contemporary regimes of truth. Similarly, the New Dealer stance's seeming predominance during McKinney Act debate was a relatively recent development, as was its apparent eclipse by talk of compassionate conservatism during the administrative tenure of George W. Bush.

Third, from the English vagrancy laws through McKinney Act debate and even up to the present, the term "work" has carried a number of connotations or expectations with it. In all cases, work appears without question to be a marker of goodness and morality. This is true for the Keeper of Order/Conservative stances and for the Reformer/Educator stances where work is used to distinguish between the deserving and the undeserving. But it is also true for the New Dealer/Liberal stances, where work is the preferred solution for resolving economic crises and restoring personal and moral self-worth. In fact, my narrative of the development of each of these regimes of truth suggests that over time, work and morality or justice have become conflated. Today, most Americans would most likely agree without reflection that work is good in and of itself and that it "builds character."

In effect, work functions as an ideograph. Indeed, work has been shown to warrant the use of power (e.g., imprisonment in the case of vagrants and/or panhandlers or marking of beggars with special identifying clothing). Work has been used to excuse behavior and beliefs which might otherwise be perceived as eccentric or antisocial (e.g., breaking up families by sending the children of poor and homeless persons to boarding schools). Work has been shown to guide behavior and belief into channels easily recognized by a community as acceptable and laudable (e.g., requiring homeless and poor aid recipients to attend sermons at alms-houses or to participate in Alcoholics Anonymous meetings).

Finally, while the terms "homeless" and "homelessness" may not be as evocative as the ideograph, "work," these terms do call forth certain images and elicit particular reactions (e.g., recall the town meeting in Santa Barbara). In effect, as evidenced by the preceding analysis, the indigent and poor—and by extension, the homeless—have been characterized in a negative light for so long that these negative characterizations appear to be inherent qualities of the poor and homeless. In particular, the homeless and homelessness seem to suggest vagrancy and thus criminality. Furthermore, they seem to intimate personal failing, laziness, and moral decay. Unfortunately, despite overt efforts to change these negative characterizations and to challenge these stereotypes, they appear especially resistant to change. As Eric Brosch explains:

> A decade ago, when America was engaged in a genuine debate over the plight of the homeless, media images of tattered figures begging for change and sleeping on heating grates were omnipresent. Apparently debate is over; today the public wants the homeless out of sight and out of mind, and legislators have responded to our waning sympathy in kind. (1998, p. 58)

Chapter Five
Science and Homelessness

If we adopt the theory of evolution (and at the present time the lay public must bow to the almost unanimous opinion of scientific men), we must be struck by the fact that through the differentiation of species arises from the cumulative perpetuation of slight differences, yet throughout nature there exists among the members of the same species a large measure of equality. (MacKay, 1889, p. 3)

If these ideas be destined, as I believe they are, to be more and more firmly established as the world grows older; if that spirit [the ethical spirit inculcated by science] be fated, as I believe it is, to extend itself to all departments of human thought, and to become co-extensive with the range of knowledge; if, as our race approaches maturity, it discovers, as I believe it will, that there is but one kind of knowledge and but one method of acquiring it, then we, who are still children, may justly feel it our highest duty to recognize the advisableness of improving natural knowledge, and so to aid ourselves and our successors in our course towards the noble goal that lies before mankind. (Thomas Huxley, reprinted in Greene, 1981, pp. 143–4)

The foundation of all knowledge is the direct observation of facts; by applying thought to the facts thus observed, we seek through a process of classification and comparison for the causes of which the observed phenomena are the results, and the conclusions thus obtained constitute science. (Strachey, 1888, p. 149)

As suggested in chapter 3, a sense of science and an often uncritical acceptance of scientific expertise serve as backdrops against which various perspectives on homelessness are developed and reproduced. However, science is not a unified institution. Perceptions of science differ between scientists and consumers of science. Furthermore, there are competing ideas of science within the scientific community itself. These differences are sometimes reflected in contemporary discussion of homelessness. In addition, a number of now defunct "sciences" seem to find new life in or faintly underpin some views of the homeless and poor.

Still, science seems to hold a privileged position in our society, one that commands the attention and efforts of most, if not all, parties involved in public policy deliberation, including deliberation on policy addressing homelessness. For example, recall Reverend Conway's testimony before the U.S. subcommittee on the Urgent Relief for the Homeless Act of 1987 presented earlier. He testified that only one scientific study on the homeless had been conducted to date and that it was flawed. He implied that because of this, " . . . there is no real understanding of the problem" (reported in Committee on Banking, 1987, p. 79). By his actions, Conway suggests that scientific knowledge, whether accurate or not, carries great weight in our society and that it cannot be ignored. Indeed, scientifically produced knowledge is apparently so highly esteemed that he felt compelled to publicly take issue with the only scientific study undertaken to date.

Based upon his subcommittee testimony (appearing in Committee on Banking, 1987, pp. 79–82) and his position as administrator for Catholic Charities, it is clear that Reverend Conway is an advocate for homeless relief and that he is committed to reducing the oppression that the homeless experience. In terms of the three contemporary positions on homelessness evident in debate surrounding the McKinney Act, Conway is a Liberal. Therefore, his concerns and his implicit desire for a more accurate scientific account of the homeless raise a number of questions pertinent to the development of a critical theory of homelessness. What role do scientific studies and science play in shaping homeless policy like the McKinney Act legislation? What notions of science facilitate this role? And given the answers to these questions, can science further critical theory's emancipatory goals?

With these questions in mind, this chapter reviews science's role in the debate on homelessness and poverty. First, I present some examples of how social scientific knowledge and scientific expertise affected the creation and implementation of the McKinney Act. Second, I briefly compare the popular views of science underlying discussion surrounding the McKinney Act with the views of science presented by those who study what scientists actually do (philosophers of science). Third, I outline a number of early scientific and prescientific notions that partially shape contemporary knowledge of homelessness. Finally, I offer some preliminary observations and tentative suggestions concerning a more democratic role for science and expertise in future policy consideration.

SCIENCE AND KNOWLEDGE OF THE HOMELESS

Scientific knowledge of topics related to the homeless and the very notion of science itself greatly affected the McKinney Act on a number of levels. An attentive reading of the McKinney Act, its related acts, and discussion surrounding these measures provides insight into the role science played in its creation. Moreover, a detailed reading of the McKinney Act affords us a view—albeit an indirect one—of the importance we accord science and of a number of scientific perspectives and strategies at play in contemporary society.

The preamble of the McKinney Act explicitly presents elderly homeless, handicapped homeless, and homeless families with children as deserving subgroups of the homeless. Similarly, various provisions of the McKinney Act distinguish between different subgroups of the homeless (e.g., mentally ill, children and youth, illiterate, and undereducated). The identification and existence of each of these subgroups were supported by a rapidly growing body of literature on the homeless from a variety of scientific sources. Social scientists, health care professionals including nurses and medical doctors, social workers, and other advocates conducting scientific research on the homeless produced volumes of new knowledge (Toro & McDonnell, 1992). Furthermore, the aura of professional expertise enveloping these authors and researchers bolstered the legitimacy of their claims and findings.

The sheer number of such scientific studies describing the homeless suggests that, not only is it possible to differentiate between the homeless and classify them by type, but it is also appropriate to do so. Such findings might be anticipated in part since, as Mark Donovan explains, " . . . professional groups confronting a policy problem bring their own routine categories and technical definitions to bear on the problem" (1993:22). In this way scientists and notions of science in general have facilitated the division of the homeless into the good and the bad, the deserving and the undeserving, and as Rob Rosenthal writes, into the "incompetent due to their own faults," the "incompetent due to no fault of their own," and the "competent but caught by circumstances" (1996, pp. 3–5).

Science influences the creation and implementation of public policy on the homeless on a number of other levels as well. For example, section 611 of Subtitle B of the McKinney Act, Community Mental Health Services, specifies that funds were to be granted to states that provide mental health services to the mentally ill. Similarly, section 613 of the same subtitle allocated funds for community demonstration projects for alcohol and drug treatment of homeless individuals. However, nowhere in the statute was "mental illness" defined, nor is "alcohol and drug abuse" explained. Yet, there is no accepted understanding of these phenomena within the scientific community, in fact, there is great contention among scientists and apparently a bit of personal animosity between some of "the experts."

For example, Alice Baum and Donald Burnes argue that we are a nation in denial when it comes to addressing homelessness. They write:

> The media, and people in general, rarely talk about how sick and physically disabled the homeless are. . . . Only when policymakers and their constituents accept the truth—that somewhere between 65 and 85 percent of the homeless population suffers from serious chronic alcoholism, addiction to drugs, severe chronic psychiatric disorders, or some combination of all three—will our society be able to develop programs and services that have any real potential for helping these most unfortunate Americans. (Baum & Burnes, 1993, p. 28)

Compare their comments with those of Stanton Peele. He argues:

> The addiction treatment industry is an expression of larger trends in American society. The principal trend has been our failure to stanch every social problem associated with the underclass that has evolved in the United States. Rather than address the social issues underlying ghetto deterioration, addiction policies speak primarily to middle-class anxieties. . . . Moreover, the addiction industry expresses the sense of our loss of control we have developed as a society; an anxiety brought on by our own utter incapacity to alter the trends over which we are so distraught. We have simply proved incapable of identifying correctly the sources of our most dire problems, and our tendency is to respond to our anxieties. (Peele, 1995, p. 232)

As another example, consider the ongoing controversy over the American Psychiatric Association's *Diagnostic and Statistical Manual* (DSM)—the manual serving as the basis for diagnosing all mental illness. Critic Paula Caplan argues that although the process of revising and updating this influential "scientific" manual is a highly political matter, it is not acknowledged as such (1991a, p. 164).[1]

Responding specifically to Caplan's critique, the DSM's defenders argue that Caplan does not adequately understand the procedures used to revise the manual (Frances, et al., 1991), to which Caplan responds: "I was not surprised that the major theme of the response by Allen Frances and his colleagues to my paper was that I don't 'understand' their procedures. Every time someone sees behind the Wizard of Oz's curtain, the would-be wizard says, 'You don't know what you are seeing, my dear'" (Caplan, 1991b, p. 174).

By not clearly defining mental illness or explaining what constitutes drug and alcohol addiction, federal lawmakers deferred to state and local lawmakers and agencies to set the standards determining who was mentally ill and who was a substance abuser. However, oftentimes states, and local governments did not set these standards. Instead, they relinquished decision-making authority to shelter workers and social workers who were left to make sense of the scientific knowledge produced by scientific and medical professionals.

This has important ramifications for both clients of homeless services and for the general population-at-large. Specifically, the discretionary power placed in the hands of shelter workers can have significant, and sometimes tragic, consequences for shelter and emergency services clients.[2] Guided by what is thought to be scientific expertise and knowledge, staff members at such facilities wield incredible power. For example, Carl I. Cohen and Kenneth S. Thompson write: "Often, involuntary psychiatric hospitalization is included as a key element of such a [mental health care] system" (1992, p. 817). They point out that " . . . an examination of data from Project Help in New York City—which is often cited as a model program for involuntary hospitalization . . . because of its broader definitions of dangerousness to self and others—reveals that roughly two-thirds of the homeless persons targeted for hospitalization were ultimately deemed unqualified for involuntary hospitalization" (1992, p. 820). The chance of mistakenly institutionalizing or medicating a "mentally healthy" person seems real given the ongoing debate over this issue within the psychiatric community itself.

Not only does the potential for compounding the hardships of homelessness and destitution with incarceration exist, but so too does the likelihood of infringement upon individual democratic and human rights. As Ivan Illich points out, the uneven power relationship between medical and scientific professionals and their clients gives great cause for concern. "Society has transferred to physicians the exclusive right to determine what constitutes sickness, who is or might become sick, and what shall be done to such people. Deviance is now 'legitimate' only when it merits and ultimately justifies medical interpretation and intervention" (Illich, 1977, pp. 13–14; see also Conrad & Schneider, 1985). Further developing this

theme, Deborah Stone warns of the dangers posed by the "natural" incli-
nation to transform social problems into clinical syndromes and describes
this tendency as "profoundly antidemocratic." She writes:

> The rise of clinical authority also constricts the realm of choice for
> individuals. The more clinicians define standards of healthy behavior
> . . . the smaller the realm of deliberation and choice for individuals.
> Ultimately, the most profound consequence of the rise of clinical
> authority is that it disguises or displaces conflict in the first place. Once
> a situation is defined as a matter of health and disease, or normality
> and pathology, both the problem and its treatment appear to be dic-
> tated by nature and no longer a matter of value choice and political
> resolutions. (Stone, 1993, p. 65)

Therefore, this type of scientific authority stymies political discussion by
presenting the social relations as apolitical, natural reality. By directing
attention away from the structural arrangements fostering social problems
such as homelessness, clinical authority reifies existing social relations.
Furthermore, in doing so it weakens democratic values such as reciprocity,
empowerment, fairness, and the desire to reduce oppression (cf. Dryzek
1990; 1996). In fact, it has the potential to lead to oppression, miscarriages
of justice, double standards, and hierarchical views of society.

As an example, in a Boston study of homeless respondents' perceptions
of need and willingness to use services, researchers report that "[m]ental
health care was perceived by interviewers as an unmet need for 64 percent of
all respondents, while only 24 percent of [homeless] respondents perceived
this need" (Tessler & Dennis, 1992, p. 36). Similarly, in a study conducted in
Milwaukee, people thought to need mental health services expressed little
interest in becoming involved in a mental health treatment program. Many
of those interviewed had received treatment as inpatients in the past and
were apparently disillusioned by their experience, perhaps rightfully so. Peele
points out, "While schizophrenics have shown substantial progress with
treatment geared toward improved management of daily life tasks, other
findings indicate that people show similar improvement on their own,
divorced of therapy" (1995, p. 16). Yet traditional mental health services,
with their growing emphasis on efficiency and their reliance upon psy-
chotropic drugs, are often all that are available (cf. Haas, 1990). Arguably,
policies and procedures that are open to the desires, opinions, and ideas of
clients and that empower clients by assisting them in their development of
improved daily life skills, would be less oppressive and more consistent with
democratic values (cf. Appleton, 1995).

COMPETING PERCEPTIONS OF SCIENCE

As evidenced in the examples concerning drug and alcohol addiction and the DSM, there is conflict and sometimes heated debate within the scientific community. Yet, in both sets of examples, the authors draw upon the latest offerings of medical science, psychiatry, psychology, and sociology to support their arguments. Similarly, each author has noteworthy experience, training, and credentials to support her or his position. For example, Baum has worked for poor and disadvantaged children in the fields of education, politics and public policy, and has been a drug and alcohol counselor for homeless people. Burnes has served as an education policy analyst and the executive director of a direct-services program for the poor and the homeless. Peele holds a Ph.D. and is a leading figure in the addictions field whose work is highly regarded and widely recognized.

Therefore, these differences are not the result of individual idiosyncrasies, inexperience, or poor training. Instead, these differences reflect the current state of expert and scientific knowledge on mental illness and drug and alcohol addiction in the U.S. today.[3] The two contradictory positions presented above represent the two poles of a continuum concerning the causes and solutions of social problems such as homelessness and drug addiction. Clearly, the scientific community itself does not enjoy a consensus.

Nevertheless, as evidenced in the preceding section, science and expertise played an important role in the formulation of the McKinney Act. In fact, they appear to play an increasingly important role in public policy formation generally. As Schneider and Ingram (1997) point out, policy makers sometimes turn to scientists to conduct research and offer expert advice when it is politically expedient; i.e., in situations where making a policy decision will displease an important segment of a politician's constituents—for example, where to locate a toxic waste dump, a nuclear waste repository, or even a homeless drop-in day center. In such cases, scientific research can serve as the rationale or cover for making politically unpopular decisions. In some situations, politicians may abdicate decision-making authority to scientists all together. Consider the National Science Foundation (NSF). Although the NSF is funded by the federal government, decisions concerning which projects to fund, the merit of individual research projects, and the like, are left in the hands of committees and boards staffed almost exclusively by scientists and experts in the various fields.

Yet some people appear either to miss or ignore this conflict and its significance. Fostered by unsophisticated portrayals of science in the media, in elementary and high school text books, and by some politicians, many people hold a different view of science. Think of Tom Hank's movie, *Apollo 13*. This movie celebrates the ingenuity, cleverness, and ability of U. S. scientists to overcome seemingly intractable problems (cf. Dennis, 1996). Similarly, Disneyland's "Tomorrowland" presents an image of a future (utopian?) society enjoying the benefits of science and technology. Likewise, the Star Wars Initiative (SWI) of the 1980s and early 1990s, and its reincarnation as the Strategic Defense Initiative in the 2000s: according to President Reagan, promised scientifically/technologically produced world peace.

Such portrayals promote a particular view of science. From this perspective, scientists methodically work through the processes of empirical observation and trial-and-error experiments to arrive at an accurate or true knowledge of reality (recall the comments of Huxley and Strachey presented at the beginning of this chapter). In particular, proponents of this view hold that there is one universal method which distinguishes scientific knowledge from other lesser forms of knowledge such as intuition and mysticism. According to this unsophisticated perspective, scientists develop theories based upon their observations and test their theories by looking for anomalies. Those theories that cannot explain anomalies are debunked or falsified. The result of employing this method is thought to be progress. Ultimately, this understanding is thought to lead to a better world—recall Thomas Huxley's remarks presented at the start of this chapter. Ronald D. Brunner and William Ascher discuss the implications of such popular notions of science for public policy in terms of a "positivistic myth." They write that those who hold or employ this myth assume that:

1. The overriding purpose of science is prediction with precision, scope, and accuracy, including prediction of the consequences of policy alternatives.
2. Such science-based predictions are prerequisites to major policy decisions intended to ameliorate or solve the problems of society.
3. Scientists are different from others who participate in these decisions because their scientific input is objective and value-free. (1992, p. 296)

Perhaps when viewed in light of these popular notions of science and scientific method—what some call "normal science"—the discord and conflict present in the examples on the DSM and on drug and alcohol addiction is unsettling. In fact, some may question whether effective public policy can be designed to address social problems such as these given the lack of consensus among social scientists and researchers. But situations in which experts and scientists hold differing, even adversarial, positions are not unusual. A number of philosophers of science and political scholars have argued that such conflict is a normal part of the politics of science.

As implied earlier, contemporary notions of science are indebted in varying degrees to the scientific enterprises preceding them. Writing of the predominant view of science in 1962, Thomas Kuhn argues: "That image has previously been drawn, even by scientists themselves, mainly from the study of finished scientific achievements as these are recorded in the classics and, more recently, in the textbooks from which each new scientific generation learns to practice its trade" (1970, p. 1). Joseph Mali describes this perspective as "a Liberal-positivist ideology of science," and he suggests that it is predicated on the "myth of rationalism" (1989, p. 145). He explains:

> According to that ideology, scientific knowledge and progress flow from free-thinking individuals who, as opposed to traditionalists, observe the phenomena objectively, seemingly unconstrained by any preestablished conceptions, or prejudices, and can thus reason securely from the raw sense-data of their experience to correct theories. (Mali, 1989, p. 143)

I would add only a positive value component, what John Dryzek and others call objectivism, to the list of the Liberal-positivist ideology of science's characteristics. By this, I mean a willingness or perhaps an unconscious predisposition on the part of those who subscribe to a "Liberal-positivistic" notion of science to defer uncritically to science and scientific expertise, what has come to be described as scientism.[4]

Rather than an objective enterprise undertaken by individuals, Kuhn argues that "normal science" typically involves communities of scientists working within a specific, shared theoretical framework on agreed upon objects of inquiry (1970, p. 5). He labels such frameworks "paradigms" and describes such communities as "paradigmatic." He also argues that "[s]cientific fact and theory are not categorically separable, except perhaps within a single tradition of normal-scientific practice" (1970, p. 7). Counter to views of normal science, Kuhn challenges the idea that scientifically derived theories are falsified when they fail to explain new observations. Instead, anomalies are "explained" through slight modification of the theory. Furthermore, he argues that methodology cannot be the source of a universal demarcation criterion for distinguishing science from non-science. Any such criterion is inherently political in nature since it is determined by the proponents of a particular paradigm and not by any set of universal principles.

Building upon Kuhn's notion of paradigm, Imre Lakatos offers his own "research programme." Rather than a community based upon a single theory, a research programme centers on a series of successive theories, each sharing common core assumptions which are not directly criticizable (Lakatos, 1978). Arguing for a conceptualization even broader than Lakatos's research program, Larry Laudan posits his own "research tradition." A research tradition also has a conceptual core, a common language which allows proponents of that tradition to communicate and speak with and to critique one another's work. He writes that it is " . . . a set of general assumptions about the entities and processes in a domain of study, and about the appropriate methods to be used for investigating the problems and constructing the theories in that domain" (Laudan, 1977, p. 89).

In answer to his critics and would-be elaborators, Kuhn acknowledges that there is a deeper sense of paradigm at work in his argument (1970, p. 185). He explains that a paradigm entails more than just shared assumptions concerning methodology and important questions; it also entails a common view of the nature of reality. At a fundamental level, scientific paradigms require that community members share the same worldview. He explains that requiring science students to work through the same repetitious exemplary problems facilitates the development of what he terms "acquired similarity relations," that is, the ability or predisposition to look for and conceptualize the world through certain similarities (1970, pp. 188–90). As already suggested, however, by no means are these similarities grounded in some necessary or universal principle.

This process is not only applicable to the hard sciences. Social scientists and philosophers of science employ similar methods and privilege certain assumptions themselves. As Rivka Feldhay and Yehuda Elkana explain:

> the hidden assumptions of a certain discourse in the 'studies of science,' common to Merton . . . Mertonian, Marxian and Weberian sociologists, Sartonian historians, Popperian and Kuhnian philosophers—all share a rather a narrow definition of the boundaries of science, stressing its rational-empirical character; implicitly or explicitly they all share the belief in the Scientific Revolution as the privileged narrative of the origins of modern science; hence they tend to tie up this story with their professional identity. (1989, p. 5)

Clearly there are significant differences between normal science and the understandings of science advanced by Kuhn, Lakatos, and Laudan. For lay people, some claims offered during debate on homelessness may appear to be grounded in notions of normal science. Returning to a previous example, claims that many of the homeless are insane may reinforce ideas that there is a clear divide between deviance in the form of insanity and normalcy. When such claims explicitly or implicitly make reference to scientific studies, but do not explicitly make reference to the contingent state of scientific knowledge about mental illness, the cultural institutions and social relations that allow some behavior to be viewed as sane or normal and other behavior as insane or abnormal are masked. In this way, views of normal science and the aura of scientific expertise reify some existing relations. In this example, mentally ill homeless people are made to appear natural and ahistorical. In addition, such claims also further the association of homelessness and insanity in general (cf. Foucault, 1965).

But more than this, such uncritical associations and implicit acceptance of a natural order can be offered in support of authoritarian policies and regimes. As suggested earlier, many of the assumptions underlying the Liberal-positivistic ideology of science seem intricately tied up with the Enlightenment meta-narrative. In particular, the belief that normal science uncovers the truth and therefore results in progress overlaps the Enlightenment meta-narrative's own promise of progress. This has significant consequences since great sacrifices can be asked or demanded of people in the name of progress.

For example, thoughts of a scientifically uncovered natural order have facilitated claims that there is an Aryan master race, thus providing a rationale for a multitude of Nazi policies and atrocities. Similarly, claims that Marxism was scientific and accurately predicted the inevitable rise of the working class were used to justify the mass starvation of millions in the Ukraine in the twentieth century. Or closer to home, the quest for scientific knowledge has been used to justify government experiments on U.S. citizens such as the syphilis experiments in Tuskegee, Alabama, from 1932 to 1972 (see Di Anni, 1993).

In contrast, the more contextualized portrayals of science made by philosophers of science do not lend themselves to such manipulation as easily. Speaking in terms of the political science discipline, Terence Ball explains:

> The framework constructed by Lakatos (and later modified by Laudan) permits us to gauge the progress of the sciences, both natural and social . . . The irony is that this approach requires rapprochement between empirical political science and normative political theory. I [suggest] that ours is a conversation consisting of many voices, each speaking in different idioms. If I am right, political science progresses

> in much the same way that a conversation progresses, and this conver-
> sation extends over time and includes not only our contemporaries but
> our ancestors as well. (1987, p. 14)

If Ball is correct and science is more accurately conceptualized as a conversation than as the application of a single, universally applicable method to
problems by essentially interchangeable practitioners (scientists), then this
has important implications for a critical theory of homelessness. A conversation entails multiple participants approaching a topic from a variety of
positions. By definition, conversation requires that participants both speak
and listen to other participants. In speaking and listening to others, participants share a degree of equality with one another and practice reciprocity.
Therefore, when conceptualized (and presented) as a conversation, science
promotes democratic values, not authoritarian values. It is harder to justify
and/or accept authoritarian measures justified by scientific evidence if science is viewed as an open-ended, less-certain process of negotiation rather
than as a univocal, universal means to uncover the truth (cf. Capra, 1975).

THE EVOLUTION (?) OF SCIENCE'S KNOWLEDGE
OF THE HOMELESS

Many have suggested that science's role in the creation and implementation
of contemporary public policy has its roots in a change in attitude concerning our (human beings') most basic relationship with ourselves and with
the exterior world (Greene, 1971; Capra, 1982; Hall, 1994; cf. Feldhay &
Elkana, 1989, p. 5). As Erwin Schrödinger explains, counter non-scientific
attitudes, this new attitude, was founded upon the belief " . . . *that the dis-
play of Nature can be understood*" (1996). This change in perception dates
back at least to the sixteenth-century work of René Descartes and his rein-
troduction of the notion of the Archimedean point and the start of the tra-
jectory of foundationalism (see Burtt, 1955; Rorty, 1979). Closer to the
subject of this work, Foucault (1965) explains that the institutions, institutional rationality, and institutional power relationships revolving around
the notion of insanity are, similarly, not timeless. He alludes to premodern
eras when justification for laws and policies permitting the internment or
punishment of the pauper, the fool, the homeless, or the political usurper
was based on coercive force, divine right of kings, or a moral order, and
not on scientific rationales (cf. Dean, 1990). Foucault writes:

> Beginning from those economic and demographic processes which
> appear clearly at the end of the 16th century, when the problem of the

poor, of the homeless, of fluctuating populations, is posed as an economic and political problem . . . an attempt is made to resolve it with an
arsenal of implements and arms (the laws concerning the poor, the more-
or-less forced isolation and, finally, imprisonment of these people. . . .
(1989, p. 186)

Sixteenth & Seventeenth Century Science

In this premodern era, the mystical and the scientific were not easily distinguished. For example, Marie Boas Hall explains:

> Scientists of the fifteenth century saw nothing 'unscientific' about an
> interest or competence in essentially linguistic matters, and in editing
> Greek scientific texts they saw themselves aiding both science and
> humanism. Indeed, science was not, as yet, a recognized independent
> branch of learning. Scientists were mostly scholars, physicians or magi-
> cians. (1994, p. 19)

She continues: "Mystic science was, in this period, the most widely known:
astrology catered for the masses by whom it was so readily understood
that in the popular mind astrologer and astronomer were one. The
alchemist's dream, too, was widely known" (1994, p. 21).

As a specific policy example, consider England's statute of 1531, "How
Aged Poor and Impotent Persons compelled to live by alms shall be ordered"
(22 Hen. VIII., c.12). Among other things, it prohibited itinerant professors
from practicing "'physiognomy, palmistry, or other crafty sciences'" (reprinted
in Ripton-Turner, 1887, p. 75). Ripton-Turner explains that "[p]hysiognomy
was a method of prediction founded upon an examination of lineaments, and
the colour and appearance of the veins" (1887, p. 75). Clearly, the need to
prohibit such crafty sciences is evidence that they were practiced widely. He
lists the following other crafty sciences in practice at the time:

> *Metoposcopy,* or judging of things to come by aspect of the forehead;
> *Æromancy,* or divination by figures in the air; *Alectromany,* or divina-
> tion by a cock; *Aruspicy,* by signs appearing in the bowels of sacrificed
> animals; *Augury,* by the flight or chattering of birds or the voices of
> animals; *Chrisallomancy,* by the lots of numbers; *Clidomancy,* by a
> key; *Corilomancy,* by a forked rod; *Coscinomancy,* by turning a sever;
> *Dactilomancy,* by a ring; *Geomancy,* by figures or lines drawn on the
> earth . . . *Hydromancy,* by appearances in the water; *Necromancy,* by
> using blood and writing or speaking certain verses for the purpose of
> raising the dead to speak and teach future things; *Onychomancy* . . .
> by the fingernails of an unpolluted boy; *Pyromancy,* by forms appear-
> ing in the fire. . . . (Ripton-Turner 1887, pp. 77–78)

Consider also the following excerpt from Richard Saunders' *Palmistry, the Secrets thereof disclosed* (1664).

> Having thus far asserted the laudable utility of *Christian Prudent Science,* let me warn my *Reader* of those *Sycophants,* and *Delusive Ignorants,* through whose *Sides* this *pretious Science* is dayly wounded, such *spawn* of *shame,* that impudently make Profession of Art, not onely in several *Countryes,* but lurk in *Obscure corners,* in and about this Famous City, many *Illiterate* pieces of *Non-scence* and *Impudence,* of the Female kind, whose Ignorance transcends the Vulgar . . . But for the *time* to *come,* that our Country may be *undeceiv'd,* I will premise such *Quallifications* as every *able Artist* ought to be indued with, according to the approbation of the best *Learned* and *Judicious,* which will serve as a *Touch stone* to examine every *Professor,* and to discern the *Prudent* from the *Impudent.*

1. The first Quallification requiste to constitute an *Artist* is, that he be highly *ingenious.*
2. Is required, a good and strong memory.
3. That he be *Prudent, Discreet, Honest,* and of a *Good* and sound judgment.
4. That he chiefly value and esteem the *Truth in* and *above* all things.
5. That he be a good *linguist* and *Scholler.*
6. That he be a good *Phylosopher,* skil'd in all parts of Phylosophy, viz. *Logick, Physicks, Ethicks,* and *Metaphisiques.*
7. That he be well *verst* in the *Stars;* their *Natures, Motions* and *Accidents,* viz. be a good *Astronomer.*
8. That he be a *Good* and *able Arithmetition.*
9. That he be a Diligent *Hearer* and *Observer* of the most Eminent Persons in his time . . .
10. That he be assiduously *Diligent* in Studies and Labours wholly intent upon the art.
11. That he be sedulously *diligent* in Collecting, Recording, and Observing all practical experiments.
12. It's very requisite that he be furnished with a meet knowledge of *agriculture* . . .

> These Quallifications *premised,* will sufficiently *inform* such of the *forfeit* of their *Judgments, Reason,* and *Discretions,* that heed *Babbling* Women and *Obscure* Persons, *Seducers,* the very *shame* and *bane* of Science. (reprinted in Ripton-Turner, 1887, pp. 75–76)

In comparison to many contemporary notions of science, Saunder's work presents many mixed messages. First, science was considered an art at the time. But many in our society view science and art as distinct, and in fact, it is common to privilege science over art. Notice that calls for greater U.S. austerity more often target the National Endowment for the Arts and the National Endowment for the Humanities for elimination, not the National Science Foundation. Second, the scientist/artist was a generalist with a wide variety of interests, not a specialist as many scientists are today. However, the scientist did have a prescribed method to follow in the pursuit of his, not her, art. Third, to accept scientific principles was rational, to be influenced by other perspectives was foolish. Fourth, science was clearly a masculine endeavor. In fact, when considered along side the rhetoric of Sir Francis Bacon, science clearly appears to be misogynistic (see Merchant, 1980; cf. Harding, 1986).[5] Finally, science was one of a number of competing perspectives about nature and our relationship to nature. In fact, the tone of Saunder's work and the voracity of his attacks on non-scientific knowledge suggest that science did not hold a privileged position; i.e., science was not established—it was still fighting for recognition.

Indeed, many have suggested that scientific explanations and scientific rationales for human behavior are relatively recent phenomena. For example, John Greene writes:

> Philosophy and theology were the main forms taken by the search for rational understanding or reality before the seventeenth century. Newton's great treatise was entitled *Mathematical Principles of Natural Philosophy*, and the science of mechanics it set forth was intimately bound up with a mechanical philosophy of nature, compounded of Greek atomism, Platonic mathematicism, and static Christian creationism. (1981, pp. 2–3)

As another example, Robert Merton describes the spread of science and technology in England during the latter half of the seventeenth century (1938). He argues that Puritanism, as opposed to the traditionalism of Catholicism, facilitated this growing interest. Contemporary commentator J. L. Heilbron reports that "Merton located the primary cause of the quickening of English interest in science in a Puritan ethic, which instilled self-reliance, sobriety, hard work, confidence in reason and experience, concern with the practical and applied, in short a dozen virtues useful to a scientist or an engineer" (1989, p. 10; cf. Weber, 1996).[6] Therefore, prior to and even contemporaneously—given the influence of Catholicism—with this quickening, some traditional or "prescientific" knowledge system(s) must have informed explanations and rationales. Indeed, Mali suggests that the three most prominent men of the scientific revolution, Francis Bacon,

Robert Boyle, and Isaac Newton, all subscribed to the "myth of the origin;" that is, "the belief that God had once revealed the truth of natural reality to humans, or at least made it accessible to them as long as their minds were innocent and therefore still capable of receiving immediate impressions without prejudice . . ." (Mali, 1989, p. 154). In essence, the "founding fathers" of science themselves relied upon a moral order to ground or rationalize science.

Nineteenth & Early Twentieth Century Science

By the nineteenth century, science was no longer the revolutionary doctrine it was during Bacon or Newton's time.[7] Rather, it had become acceptable, if not routine, and was practiced widely throughout the modern or "civilized" world. Accordingly, numerous scientific enterprises and sciences of a dubious and often unsavory nature were undertaken throughout the nineteenth century. Among these were the related and often mutually-reaffirming sciences, Phrenology and Social Darwinism. Today, echoes of these sciences still can be heard reverberating in contemporary rhetoric and debate concerning homelessness.

Phrenology, at its most base level, was the physiological study of skulls, cranial shapes and human brains. Note the parallels between phrenology and the sixteenth century's physiognomy and palmistry. In phrenology, it was assumed that there was a correlation between an individual's behavior and/or characteristics and the ascribed normality or abnormality of that individual's brain. Phrenology's proponents presented it as a means of answering almost all social ills. For example, Professor Moriz Benedikt's phrenological study, *Anatomical Studies Upon the Brains of Criminals*, sought a scientific basis or corollary for criminal behavior— in this case, unusual features on the surface of criminals' brains (1881, p. viii). As the editors of the 1971 reissue of the book explain: "With a clear anatomical knowledge of patterns typical among criminal brains, it would be possible to refine criminology into a more exact and predictable science. . . . Were it possible to recognize physical defects and depraved tendencies . . . individual security could almost be entirely guaranteed" (Benedikt,1881, p. VI). And Benedikt did "recognize physical defects" in the brain. He writes:

> There remains nothing more, for the present at least, but to express the proposition: THE BRAINS OF CRIMINALS EXHIBIT A DEVIATION FROM THE NORMAL TYPE, AND CRIMINALS ARE TO BE VIEWED AS AN ANTHROPOLOGICAL VARIETY OF THEIR SPECIES. AT LEAST AMONG THE CULTURED RACES.

> This proposition is calculated to create a veritable revolution in Ethics, psychology, jurisprudence, and criminalistics. (1881, p. 157)

However, phrenology did not live up to its promise. Even at the height of its influence and preeminence, serious proponents of the science had cause for concern. In his first public address as University Chair of Phrenology at Anderson University in Glasgow, Scotland, delivered in 1846, Andrew Coombe warned:

> it is to warn you that it is of Phrenology as it exists in the minds of the well-informed cultivators, after years of study and observation, that I speak, and not of the fancy which many substitute for it in their minds, and designate by its name. Of the latter kind of Phrenology, nobody can have a lower opinion than I have. It neither is nor ever can be of any use, either to its possessor or to others. The Phrenology which I have here recommended to you, is a science which cannot be mastered or judged of in a day, in a week, or in a month. Like other sciences, it must be studied before it is known. Many entertain the notion that they have only to read a book or a pamphlet to qualify themselves to estimate its bearings, and pronounce authoritatively on its merits. This is a grand mistake. . . . (reprinted in introduction to Coombe, 1834, pp. x-xi)

Certainly one of phrenology's "grand mistakes" was the part it played in the establishment and maintenance of scientific racism, the effects of which are still experienced today. For instance, although we know scientifically that race has no substantive biological basis—indeed, scientists report that there is greater genetic diversity between members of the same so-called races than there is between the races themselves—many scientists continue to uncritically use race as a variable in their research (Tashiro, 1996). This is not to suggest that people do not experience racism, bigotry, and oppression because of their racial appearance. However, to uncritically use race as a variable without overtly proclaiming it to be grounded in social convention rather than in biological laws or physiological reality reifies race as a natural feature of human beings. Accordingly, the "seemingly" inherent characteristics dividing humans into racial groups supports the process of differentiation as discussed in chapter 2. In this way, uncritically employing race as a variable makes racism, bigotry, and oppression based on different physical appearances possible.

For example, consider the term "welfare queen." Put into circulation during the Reagan administration, the phrase quickly gained widespread currency in U.S. popular culture. It is a pejorative term used to describe those women who live the good life at the taxpayers' expense (see Hackey & Whitehouse, 1996, p. 22; see also *Harvard Law Review*, 1994). However, because many people believe race to be a biological reality and an important explanatory variable, the term "welfare queen" was easily racialized. Unfortunately, for many the label elicited images of Black women on welfare having children out of wedlock to increase the size of their welfare checks—disregarding the fact that no one lived high off the meager allowances provided by welfare; participation in welfare programs was based on one's economic circumstances, not one's race, and those who claimed that women have additional children in order to increase their welfare payments often base their claims *only* on anecdotal evidence.

As Evelyn Brodkin points out, President Reagan often cited a handful of welfare abuse cases repeatedly to support his attempts to undercut support for welfare policies. Press secretary David Geren justified Reagan's behavior, calling Reagan's stories "political parables." Brodkin disparagingly labels these parables "symbolic truths," and she points out that although President Reagan offered no evidence to back his inflammatory claims, they were still incredibly influential (Brodkin, 1993, pp. 647–649). Indeed, the speed with which welfare queen's usage became acceptable suggests that Reagan's political parables tapped into a deeply ingrained cultural nerve. As a society we appear to have a predisposition for this type of imagery and conception. Our readiness to judge and condemn others according to character and racial type may be facilitated by common sense knowledge of distinct biological races and character types promoted by amateur phrenologists, by the science of phrenology, and by naive notions of science in general.

Advocates of what has come to be identified as Social Darwinism also presented it as a positive, life-improving science. Social Darwinism arose as a number of relatively new beliefs concerning the nature of the universe came into fashion. Among these were: the belief in the evolution of organic matter from the simplest to the most complex living forms; a quasi-religious belief in the free market, which, if allowed to operate freely, would act as guarantor of natural liberty and would assure the progress of Humankind; the belief that the laws governing human progress were analogous to those governing the physical world; and finally, the rejection of the emotive, intuitive, or traditional basis of knowledge in favor of knowledge founded on empirical sensory experience. The convergence of these perspectives facilitated the consecration of laissez-faire political-economic policy as a "science," i.e., Social Darwinism. For example, in his 1889 book, *The English Poor*, Thomas MacKay argued that the "modern doctrine of Evolution" supports an individualistic basis of society (1889, p. vii). He explains:

By Individualism is meant the rule of conduct which obliges each individual man to adapt his instincts, habits, and character to his surroundings. These surroundings in civilised and associated life are governed by economic laws, which though not of inflexible rigidity are yet more permanent in their nature than human character. They are indeed the environment in reference to which human character must be formed. The definition assumes that man has inherited a capacity for this course of action, a capacity which can be developed by use and transmitted with ever-growing intensity to successive generations. This to the Individualist is Nature's Covenant of Progress. (1889, p. vi)

Drawing upon examples like this, Greene explains:

Social theory is 'biologized' by means of an analogy between the competitive struggle in society and the 'stern discipline of Nature' in the biological realm, and physics, biology, and sociology are united in an evolutionary world view combining the mechanical philosophy of the seventeenth century with the idea of progressive development in natural history and the laissez-faire doctrines of British political economy. Science, ideology, and world view are interfused. (1981, p. 6; cf. Thoughts and facts contributing to the history of Man, 1864)[8]

This marriage of economic policy and science proved the perfect justification for a whole host of social practices such as the continuation of colonialism, Western and Japanese imperialism, the science of Eugenics, and the forced sterilization of indigenous people and people of color. For example, Darwin argued:

the weak members of civilised societies propagate their kind. No one who has attended to the breeding of domestic animals will doubt that this must be highly injurious to the race of man. It is surprising how soon a want of care, or care wrongly directed, leads to the degeneration of a domestic race; but excepting in the case of man himself, hardly any one is so ignorant as to allow his worst animals to breed. (Darwin, 1896, p. 134)

Or consider Alfred Wallace's claim:

When the power that had hitherto modified the body [natural selection], transferred its action to the mind, then races would advance and become improved merely by the harsh discipline of a sterile soil and inclement seasons. Under their influence, a hardier, a more provident, and a more social race would be developed, than in those regions where the earth produces a perennial supply of vegetable food, and where neither foresight nor ingenuity are required to prepare for the rigours of winter.

It is the same great law of *'the preservation of favoured races in the struggle for life,'* which leads to the inevitable extinction of all those low and mentally underdeveloped populations with which Europeans come in contact. (1864, pp. clxiv-v)

Such rhetoric reverberated in debate over the McKinney Act, just as it continues to reverberate in more recent calls for welfare reform. Today, many Conservatives vocally criticize homeless and social welfare policy itself because they argue that it has a debilitating effect on aid recipients (e.g., see Murray, 1984). In essence, they argue that such federal policies foster a culture of poverty.[9] Critics charged that such policies led aid recipients to believe that they could not escape their circumstances through their own efforts, thus leading them to give up attempts to better themselves. Others charged that welfare state policies were so generous that they enticed recipients to stay on the dole. Even some moderate Democrats, evidently not wanting to "blame the victim," claimed that welfare recipients and indigents were victims of a faulty system—a system which prevented them from facing adversity, from "taking their licks." Hence, welfare recipients were denied the chance to learn from their experiences.

From this perspective, the appropriate solution to homelessness and poverty appears to be the removal of the "unnatural" barriers which prevent the poor from succeeding or failing of their own accord. In effect, this perspective is predicated on the assumption that the injustice of poverty and indigence resides not in the actual conditions of poverty which are apparently inevitable, but in the denial of those on welfare the opportunity to fail on their own (cf. Lakoff, p. 1996). Perhaps Howard Pyle, aide to U.S. President Dwight Eisenhower, said it best, "The right to suffer is one of the joys of a free economy" (1995).

Darwin and Wallace's arguments dovetail nicely with, or perhaps drive late nineteenth- and early twentieth-century psychologists' and criminologists' preoccupation with developing oral and written tests to determine delinquency, feeble-mindedness, criminality, and employability (e.g., see Pinter & Toops, 1917; 1918; Johnson, 1917). As Hazel M. Cushing and G. M. Ruch so aptly explain: "It is unnecessary to take space to comment at length upon the usefulness of character measurements which will select potential delinquents and incorrigibles prior to the commission of acts which are subject to the actions of the courts" (1927, p. 1). It was unnecessary because this view was apparently widely held and common sensical.

Finally, one other, less ignoble trend involving science merits attention here. By the late nineteenth century and the early twentieth century, a more vulgarized conception of science became fashionable. From this perspective, science and the scientific were equated with efficiency and the efficient. Around this time, then, a scientific veneer was imparted to various organizational schemes. For instance, Frank Carlton writes:

> Scientific management or efficiency engineering is concerned with two somewhat interrelated matters. The first is the efficient systematization of the work in a given factory from the engineering or mechanical point of view—the routing of the work, proper cutting speeds, the care of tools and machines, and the like. The second factor is psychological in its nature; it relates to the effective methods of 'engineering' the workers by providing potent incentives and by stimulating interest in the work. (Carlton, 1912, pp. 834–835; cf. Frey, 1913, pp. 400–401)

Closer to the topic at hand, Katz (1996) points out that philanthropists of the nineteenth and early twentieth century claimed to have developed a set of experientially-based, governing principles of poverty, charity, and relief, otherwise known as "scientific charity." Leading philanthropist Lowell wrote: "The task of dealing with the poor and degraded has become a science, and has its well defined principles, recognized and conformed to, more or less closely, by all who really give time and thought to the subject" (1884, p. I). Ultimately, scientific charity focused upon the most efficient distribution of aid to the deserving poor and unfortunate and an emphasis on finding the proper incentive to motivate the poor to work. The spread of such bare-bones notions of science has played a major role in today's political climate and especially in today's policy formation arena. Certainly such notions play a substantial role in contemporary calls for states rights, in calls for further dismantling of federal welfare-related policies, and in calls to privatize social services in order to more efficiently—read more scientifically—manage government (cf. Browdin, 1997).

DISCUSSION

As suggested earlier, the turn to scientific expertise in deciding public policy on social issues such as homelessness is cause for concern at a number of levels. At the most immediate level, through our willingness to uncritically defer to science or scientists, we maintain our ignorance and confusion in what are ultimately political matters (Illich, 1977; Stone, 1993). In doing so we disempower ourselves and become dependent upon an elite caste—scientists, health care officials, psychiatrists, and psychologists. Such dependence is clearly undesirable (cf. Kyle, 2004). Recall that phrenology and eugenics were once cutting-edge science. Or consider that there is always the possibility that an individual may become homeless and experience the fate sketched in the first substantive section of this chapter (e.g., involuntary institutionalization).

At an intermediate level, scientific research and expertise are employed in the creation of specific policies directed at the homeless. However, such policies often appear to promote the social status quo by focusing attention on the individual or group level, thus masking structural relations that result in some homelessness. As Susan Yeich explains:

> Government has catered to the interests of elite groups not only by implementing conservative policies, but by propagating conservative ideology which has served to justify inequality and keep impoverished people docile and self-blaming.

> Social science research has played a major role in propagating this idea. Numerous research studies have examined 'deviant' characteristics of homeless people, such as mental illness and substance abuse, and defined these characteristics as the causes of homelessness. These research findings provided policy-makers with a rationale for the growing homelessness problem and a justification for ignoring the structural conditions giving rise to the problem. (1994, p. 26)

At an even more abstract level, the rise of scientism, and perhaps even the scientific meta-narrative itself, facilitates the development and spread of anti-democratic beliefs and values. Writing in 1950, Adorno et al. argue that the following characteristics constitute a 'more or less central trend' in the authoritarian personality.

a. *Conventionalism.* Rigid adherence to conventional, middle-class values.
b. *Authoritarian submission.* Submissive, uncritical attitude toward idealized moral authorities of the ingroup.
c. *Authoritarian Aggression.* Tendency to be on the lookout for, and to condemn, reject, and punish people who violate conventional values.
d. *Anti-intraception.* Opposition to the subjective, the imaginative, the tender-minded.
e. *Superstition and stereotypy.* The belief in mystical determinants of the individuals fate; the disposition to think in rigid categories.
f. *Power and 'toughness.'* Preoccupation with the dominance-submission, strong-weak, leader-follower dimension; identification

with power figures; overemphasis upon the conventional attributes of ego; exaggerated assertion of strength and toughness.

g. *Destructiveness and cynicism.* Generalized hostility, vilification
of the human.

h. *Sex.* Exaggerated concern with sexual 'going-ons.' (1950, p. 228)

Building upon such work, Dryzek argues that instrumental rationality may
often foster anti-democratic values. He explains that democratic societies
experience a tension between a desire for rationality and egalitarian principles. "A further threat to democracy arises because individuals reduced to
calculating machines are susceptible to totalitarian appeals promising to
restore meaning to their lives" (1990:5).

Accordingly, emphasizing or repeatedly calling attention to the supposed individual failings of homeless and destitute persons—in this case
the psychological problems and/or drug dependence often associated with
homelessness—can foster an attitude of contempt for those less well off
and submission to those better off. Also, institutionalizing, medicating, or
incarcerating homeless under the guise of scientifically derived humanitarian relief may promote a tendency to look out for and to condemn, reject,
and punish people who violate norms. By concentrating on the differences
that separate the homeless from "us" and that separate the deserving
homeless from the undeserving homeless, lawmakers, politicians, academics and the media reaffirm these very differences and facilitate the conditions that foster authoritarian values such as compliance, rigidity,
intolerance, and cynicism.

Reflecting upon the work of Dryzek, Foucault, Illich, Stone, Adorno,
and many others, it becomes clear that scientific/medical expertise is a double-edged sword. It offers potentially useful guidance and aid, and at the
same time, when employed uncritically, it can foster undemocratic values
and relationships. Examples pointing to both edges can be found in academic literature on the homeless, in public debate over homeless policy,
and in public policies themselves. Interested parties with greatly disparate
aims and concerns are able to employ one edge of the sword of scientific
expertise, but not without being cut by the other edge.

In the case of those who support a more laissez-faire approach to
matters concerning the homeless, emphasis upon the individual failings of
the homeless—whether due to mental illness, alcoholism, drug abuse,
sociobiological factors—has been rather successful over time. In utilizing
scientific expertise and research to support their political agenda, however,
these individuals limit their own range of acceptable behavior.

On the other hand, advocates who promote widespread recognition of the heterogeneous nature of homelessness and point to those factors beyond the control of the homeless, such as economic downsizing, mental illness, or abusive family relationships, as a strategy designed to secure beneficial policies and more funding inadvertently and indirectly support those who proponents of a laissez-faire approach. By emphasizing the deserving homeless in this way, they are lending support to the notion that there are other homeless who are undeserving.

Yet critical theories themselves often employ scientific approaches to the study of social reality. Critical theories are grounded in observations of empirical reality (e.g., sign and linguistic systems, economic structures, oppressive social relations). Indeed, Marx placed great stock in science and worked conscientiously to promote his ideas as a new science. Ironically, it is perhaps a turn toward some of the more basic driving principles of the scientific method or "modern" attitude that holds the best promise for creatively and effectively overcoming some of the negative consequences of uncritically employing science. In light of the preceding discussion, reliance upon instrumental rationality and logic, emphasis on "the facts," and the desire to remain as objective as possible lead, paradoxically, to the realization that "the facts" are anything but objective. Accordingly, as we find ourselves living in a "postmodern" age in which rationality has been turned in upon itself, i.e., when rationality itself is interrogated rationally, objectively it behooves us to acknowledge that our understanding of reality is not objective. It further behooves us to admit that clinging to such modern notions as "the myth of science" (Brunner & Ascher, 1992) and our irrational demand for "an order beyond time and chance which both determines the point of human existence and establishes a hierarchy of responsibilities" (Rorty, 1989, p. xv) has very dire political consequences for all of us. If this realization were to become accepted widely, perhaps debate on social ills such as homelessness, poverty, and addiction could move beyond the us/them dichotomy that typifies "modern" discussion. Perhaps we could look at societal problems in ways that do not necessarily have winners and losers. Perhaps then we could begin to address homelessness in ways that do not recreate the conditions that foster homelessness in the first place.

Chapter Six
Conclusions and Critical Review

For we each of us deserve everything, every luxury that was ever piled in the tombs of the dead kings, and we each of us deserve nothing, not a mouthful of bread in hunger. Have we not eaten while another starved? Will you punish us for that? Will you reward us for the virtue of starving while others ate? No man [sic] earns punishment, no man earns reward. Free your mind of the idea of deserving, the idea of earning, and you will begin to be able to think. (Fictional anarchists theoretician and activist Odo, presented in Ursula K. Le Guin, 1974, p. 288)

Proletarian revolutions . . . such as those of the nineteenth century, criticize themselves in their own course; come back to what seems to have been accomplished, in order to start anew; scorn with cruel thoroughness the half measures, weaknesses and meanness of their first attempts; seem to throw down their adversary only to enable him to draw fresh strength from the earth and again rise up against them in more gigantic stature; constantly recoil in fear before the undefined monster magnitude of their own objects—until finally that situation is created which renders all retreat impossible and conditions themselves to cry out: 'Hic Rhodus, hic salta!' [Here is the rose. And here we must dance!]. (from Karl Marx's *Eighteenth Brumaire of Louis- Bonaparte*, reprinted in Rosa Luxemburg 1970, p. 89)

This project began with my interpretation of the poem, "Short Thigh," written by Peptol, a homeless man in Arizona with whom I was occasionally conversant. I was especially struck by his repeated use of the phrase "Hear we are." I read this phrase as a plea not only to recognize and acknowledge the existence of homeless individuals, but also as a call to situate the homeless historically and to deeply contextualize homelessness itself.

In answer to Peptol's call to acknowledge that "we are sharing this moment of hear we are," I turned to the tradition of critical theory for guidance and support. I did so because my analyses share some of critical theory's characteristics and because I am concerned with some of the same methodological and theoretical difficulties that many critical theorists discuss.

All critical theories share at least two goals. First, they are driven by a desire to end or reduce oppression. This involves replacing oppressive institutions, relations, and policies with unoppressive or less oppressive ones. It also involves empowering the oppressed so that they may take part in overcoming the oppression they experience. This is clearly a goal of my work. I hope that better homeless policy will result from a greater awareness of the historical and rhetorical milieu that frame people's experiences of homelessness and out of which public policies directed at the homeless arise. Furthermore, I hope that this research effort will aid in consciousness-raising among those homeless who solely blame themselves for their indigent conditions.

Second, by definition, critical theories engage in critiques of various cultural institutions, practices, social relations, and modes of thought. Through critiques, critical theories illustrate the underlying operations, conditions, relations, unacknowledged assumptions, and prejudices that sustain social ills such as poverty, homelessness, homo-prejudice, and racism. Clearly this research effort is such a project.

However, as discussed in chapter 1, critical theorists differ over some important assumptions. Among these assumptions are: (a) the implied possibility of truth; (b) the existence of a subject standing outside or prior to language and culture; (c) the notion of false consciousness; and (d) some degree of historical determinism. These differences serve as the basis for two distinct schools of critical theory, the modern school and the postmodern school. Generally speaking, postmodern critical theorists argue that each of these assumptions is potentially dangerous in that acting in accord with them may promote oppression, and therefore, they should be avoided whenever possible. In addition, postmodern critical theorists argue that some of the ideas, vocabulary, and theoretical tools that modern critical theorists employ reflect these four assumptions. Therefore, they suggest that many modern critical theories reinforce oppressive relations on one level even as they expose the underlying operation of oppressive institutions on another level.

In contrast, modern critical theorists generally are not as concerned with the negative impact of these assumptions. Furthermore, many modern critical theorists argue that postmodern critical theorists serve as agents of the status quo by refusing to offer alternatives and by undermining historical analysis.

Both schools offer particular insights that merit attention. Unfortunately, critical theorists from the two opposed camps expend great energy and effort in debate over these issues. Few critical theorists attempt to build upon the insights of the two schools; i.e., too few critical theories use the insights of both schools. My work is an attempt to bridge these two schools of critical theory. In particular, I set out to offer an extended historical and rhetorical analysis of some concepts and perspectives that made recent understanding of and attitudes toward homelessness possible.

With these goals and concerns in mind, I grounded my analyses in debate surrounding the creation and implementation of the McKinney Act. To promote a greater understanding of homelessness in the United States and to contribute to a comprehensive critical theory of homelessness, I presented a legislative history of the McKinney Act and related measures. This strategy was based upon the assumption that homelessness is largely a product of the historical relations, discourses, and rationalities at play in society. I contend that preexisting discourses, social constructions, ideographs, and narratives greatly influenced the understandings of homelessness that served as the backdrop against which the McKinney Act was crafted and implemented, just as they and the McKinney Act itself continue to influence policy addressing homelessness today. However, these are not so authoritative that they absolutely set the parameters of debate. Instead, they offer "paths of less resistance" that can guide and shape current debate on homelessness. In this way, if policies addressing homelessness are to be successful over time, their authors must take account of these discourses, earlier regimes of truth, social constructions, ideographs and narratives.

Through my account of the development of the McKinney Act, I suggested that three broad perspectives toward homelessness underlay discussion of the McKinney Act: a Conservative stance, an Educators stance, and a Liberal stance. In over-generalized terms, those individuals holding the Conservative position view the homeless as responsible for their indigent condition. Accordingly, they do not see a need for federal intervention on behalf of the homeless and poor. Those individuals arguing from the Educators stance consider the homeless to be responsible for their indigent state due to personal inadequacies; e.g., lack of marketable skills or inadequate education. However, unlike those subscribing to the Conservative stance, they believe that the federal government has a responsibility to provide assistance to the homeless so that they may overcome their inadequacies. Those individuals espousing the Liberal perspective do not view the homeless as responsible for their fate; instead, they emphasize the structural underpinnings of homelessness. Therefore, they hold that the federal government has a responsibility to aid the indigent.

I also illustrated how these three perspectives draw upon and are partially shaped by preexisting discourses. In particular, I identified four different general views of individual and state responsibility concerning the indigent: the Virtuous Christian, Keeper of Order, Reformer, and New Dealer perspectives. I argued that each of these stances roughly corresponds to a different discourse, and I suggested that these serve as the backdrop against which the McKinney Act was discussed and against which contemporary discussion of homelessness continues. To demonstrate this, I pointed out some similarities between the Keeper of Order perspective and the Conservative perspective, between the Reformer stance and the Educators stance, and between the New Dealer view and the Liberal view. In presenting these connections, I highlighted the way that notions of labor/work play a key role in defining these different perspectives. Because of this, I argued that work is an ideograph.

Furthermore, I noted the important role that science played in the creation of the McKinney Act. I discussed how science affects critical social analyses and how it may play a part in the formulation of less oppressive, more democratic, social policy. In particular, I suggested that the term science often evokes overly simplified (junior high and high school) notions of scientific method, and as such I argued that science is also an ideograph. I discussed how belief in scientific and technological progress manifests itself in the form of scientism, facilitating a sometimes-imprudent willingness to rely upon scientific expertise rather than on personal evaluation. Accordingly, I argued that science is often presented as a narrative that nicely complements the Enlightenment narrative. I also presented examples of how different notions of science and defunct sciences influenced the formulation of the McKinney Act and how they shaped earlier conceptions of poverty that in turn affected today's notions of homelessness.

IMPLICATIONS

Given the assumptions underlying my analyses, consideration of these discourses, ideographs, and narratives in relation to homelessness partially explains how the McKinney Act evolved as it did. Similarly, consideration of these factors also sheds some light on the development of related social policies. For example, as recently as the mid 1980s many—if not most—Americans accepted social welfare programs such as Aid to Families with Dependent Children (AFDC) and Supplemental Security Income (Social Security) as permanent features of the U.S. political system. Similarly, many Americans thought it natural for the federal government to address the growing homeless problem of the 1980s.

However, this situation changed dramatically in a very short time. Calls to rescind or drastically reduce welfare programs gained widespread currency during the Reagan and elder Bush administrations. The Reagan administration actively worked to diminish, if not eliminate, many social welfare programs, and its policies systematically undermined the economic foundations of these programs (see Pierson, 1994). And to the chagrin of many advocates for the homeless and many left-of-center intellectuals— myself included—social welfare policy retrenchment continued under the direction of the traditionally left-of-center Democratic Party. For example, Democratic presidential candidate Bill Clinton pledged to "end welfare as we know it" in 1992 (see Lehman & Danziger, 1995), leading to the transformation of the AFDC program into the more limited Temporary Aid to Needy Families program in 1996. Since the Clinton administration, calls to privatize the Social Security system and to further privatize Medicare seem to be gaining greater currency and legitimacy.

Yet expanding social welfare policies was the order of the day for half a century. Accordingly, these developments apparently surprised many holding the liberal perspective. In fact, these developments came so rapidly that many left-of-center intellectuals who had previously offered insightful, sometimes scathing, critiques of liberal policies rallied to defend the former status quo. For example, Frances Fox Piven, Richard Cloward, and Irving Howe, who had previously critiqued social welfare policies for the role they played in sustaining the capitalist economy and its concomitant social ills, joined in the defense of liberal policies (see Stoesz & Karger, 1992).

However, this sea change in the U.S. approach to social welfare policy does not appear so radical when considered from a more contextualized, more historically aware perspective. In fact, when viewed in light of the analyses offered in chapters 3 and 4, liberal policies toward poverty and homelessness appear to be an aberration—albeit a 50-year aberration—rather than the norm. In comparison to the discourses underpinning the Conservative and Educators stances, the discourse corresponding to the Liberal stance seems to be a relative newcomer. Therefore, it is no wonder that even at its height, there is still some question whether the Liberal stance ever achieved dominance in the U.S.

This has important implications for those seeking to address social problems such as poverty and homelessness today. For example, as discussed in chapter 3, advocates actively worked to change traditional social constructions and characterizations associated with the homeless. Indeed, the McKinney Act may be viewed as a testament to their early success. However, since its passage, the number of reports devoted to homelessness in big media outlets has substantially dropped (Guzicki & Toro, 2002; Buck, Toro & Ramos, 2004), although the number of homeless persons has not declined dramatically. Similarly, a growing number of city-level and county-level governments are enacting get-tough measures against the homeless. Yet these developments should come as no surprise, given a more historically contextualized view. Premised on the belief that it is possible to discriminate between the deserving and undeserving, negative views of the homeless made manifest in public apathy, hostility, and punitive measures are more entrenched than liberal views and policies.

This raises important concerns for the homeless, for others traditionally deemed undeserving, and for their supporters. It seems that it is not enough to create policies addressing the immediate needs of such individuals. (The sponsors of the McKinney Act admitted as much themselves). Once such policies are passed, individuals and society in general may lose interest in the problem or become frustrated when the problem persists (cf. Kinnick, 1994). This seems to be the case for the homeless crisis. Unfortunately, this disinterest and/or frustration in turn may stymie future efforts to provide additional assistance for needy individuals.

Therefore, policies addressing the conditions that facilitate homelessness must also be enacted. But accomplishing this is no easy task. The economic and social relations that lead many to experience homelessness are consistent with and reinforced by the discourse corresponding to the Conservative perspective and the regime of truth hinted at by the Keeper of Order perspective. In addition, these relations are supported by negative social constructions and characterizations of indigent people. To overcome these factors, a concerted effort to bolster the spread of the discourse associated with the Liberal perspective and to reconstruct the image of homeless persons may be required.

Given recent policy developments and shifts in national priorities, apparently 50 years of liberal policies were not sufficient to establish the Liberal perspective and its related discourse firmly. Hence, there is no radical Liberal regime of truth in place today. Clearly, the task of installing a regime of truth not based on the distinction between the deserving and undeserving or even a Liberal sensibility toward the homeless is a difficult and laborious one. However, this does not mean it is an impossible task.

As suggested in chapter 4, different discourses have ascended to prominence at times and then have receded to become resistant discourses at other times. Significant changes have occurred in the past and can occur in the future. No discourse or ideology has become so great that it entirely eclipsed resistant discourses and conflicting perspectives. Similarly, no regime of truth is eternal; they are always contested; there are always contending regimes of truth. However, the discourses corresponding to the

Keeper of Order and Conservative perspectives seem more resilient, more entrenched, than the discourse underlying the Liberal perspective.

At least two key factors lay behind this. First, these discourses are intricately related to and supported by a number of the pillars upon which contemporary Western society rests. As examples, consider Judeo-Christianity and Patriarchy.[1] In oversimplified terms, these discourses are bolstered by several strong Judeo-Christian—especially Torah/Old Testament—themes. For example, according to Biblical accounts, God sits in judgment of us, rewarding the good (deserving) and punishing the evil or wicked (undeserving). Therefore, some may offer this belief as evidence that the circumstances of particular individuals are God's will; accordingly, the homeless have no homes because they are wicked. As another example, the Torah's creation stories reports that humans were cast out of the Garden of Eden as a punishment for early humanity's disobedience. These stories tell us that God commanded that we sustain ourselves by the sweat of our brows; i.e., God commanded us to work. Accordingly, those who do not work (the stereotypical homeless person and those receiving government assistance) are disobeying God. Therefore, they are wicked and are not deserving of assistance. As a final example, consider the adage "an eye for an eye." This clearly supports a view of the world where responsibility can be decided easily and unequivocally. Each of these may serve to support the Keeper of Order and Conservative perspectives' presumption that individuals are personally responsible for their fortune or misfortune. In this way, these stories may serve to support the view that society has no responsibility to offer assistance to the unfortunate.

Again in oversimplified terms, patriarchy complements the Keeper of Order and Conservative discourses. For example, it finds support in patriarchal relations and values such as the inherent inequality of human beings; that is, men are naturally superior to women (e.g., they are physically stronger, more rational), some men are superior to other men, some women are superior to other women, and adults are superior to children. Therefore, under patriarchy, hierarchal social relations based on gender and other criteria are not only acceptable, but they are natural because of these assumed differences.[2] To contest this natural order is to ask for trouble. For example, some have presented homeless women as rebels who have challenged the naturally ordained patriarchal order—i.e., they left their husbands, they ran away from their families, and/or they had children out of wedlock. As such, they have brought their misfortune upon themselves and thus do not deserve assistance (see Harris, 1991). Such beliefs, sometimes spoken, sometimes not, seem to underlie George W. Bush's welfare reform initiative to promote marriage as a way to address social ills like poverty and child abuse (Pear & Kirkpatrick, 2004; McClain, 2002).

Similarly, given the natural inferiority of some people, some employ circular logic to define those who are unsuccessful (e.g., the homeless and welfare recipients) as inherently inferior. Accordingly, by reifying hierarchy, patriarchy may serve to support the Conservative perspective's belief that society is not responsible for the misfortunes people suffer. In very general terms, patriarchal beliefs reinforce the idea that those who suffer misfortune are naturally inferior. Thus, there is no need to make substantial changes in social, economic, or cultural relations for the homeless and indigent.

In contrast, the discourse reverberating in the Liberal perspective—especially its more radical, critical theory-related aspects—is reproduced in less pervasive, more resistant belief/value systems and political movements. For example, it is bolstered by and reflected in the various women's movements that have developed over time (see Eisler, 1987; Freedman, 2002), including the various contemporary feminisms (see Jaggar, 1983; Howard & Allen, 2000). It is supported by the utopian socialist experiments of the nineteenth and early twentieth centuries. It found expression in the Marxist-, Maoist- and social anarchist-inspired revolutions of the nineteenth and twentieth centuries. It underpinned the socialist governments of several Western European nations until very recently. And in the U.S., it is most often voiced by the authors of utopian science fiction and fantasy works (e.g., see Le Guin, 1974; 1987; Piercy, 1983).

Second, the Keeper of Order perspective has been the basis for national public laws for more than five centuries in the West. In contrast, the Liberal perspective has only found expression in federal public laws for the last five decades or so in the U.S. Accordingly, raising the Liberal perspective and discourse within which it is grounded to dominance may take centuries, not merely years or decades.

Therefore, advocates for the homeless and for others characterized as undeserving must act with two primary goals in mind. We must work to reduce the oppression and deprivation that the homeless experience in their daily lives. This entails meeting their most immediate needs: shelter, food, and medical and psychiatric attention. It entails working to empower homeless individuals through consciousness-raising, education, and skills training, so that they may act on their own behalf (see Shorris, 1997; Freire, 1970). It also entails working to eliminate the structural relations that underpin homelessness.

But we must also work to bolster the liberal discourse and reinforce the Liberal perspective if we hope to change fundamentally the relations that precipitate homelessness in the first place. In particular, we must reintroduce the more critical (radical) elements of the Liberal perspective and work to see that they are seriously considered and not dismissed out of turn as they are often today. This entails promoting the idea that we live in a post-scarcity world where everyone's needs, but not everyone's wants, can be met (see Bookchin, 1971). This goal also entails moving beyond discussion of merit and beyond labeling some deserving and others undeserving. It entails promoting notions of fraternity, solidarity, and community. However, even as we work to promote these ideals, we must continue to tirelessly critique the Liberal perspective and discourse.

Sometimes the means used to pursue these goals are complementary. However, sometimes the means employed to pursue one of these goals undercut efforts to achieve another of these goals. For example, in working to meet the immediate needs of many homeless persons, advocates worked to secure passage of the McKinney Act. To do this, advocates for the homeless actively worked to recast the overall image of the homeless in terms of the most deserving of the homeless. While successful in obtaining federal aid, this strategy worked against the goal of promoting the Liberal stance in that it reinforced the idea that there are deserving and undeserving people. Therefore, this strategy implicitly supported the distribution of aid according to perceived merit. Consistent with this distribution scheme, most of the federal aid was directed at meeting the needs of individual homeless persons; e.g., overnight shelter, emergency mental health care and medical assistance, education for homeless children and substance abuse treatment. This aid was not directed at addressing the structural underpinnings that foster the conditions of homelessness. It is ironic that pursuit of this strategy did not seriously challenge the social and economic arrangements that led many to become homeless in the first place.

Furthermore, this strategy may have empowered some homeless persons—the most well off of the homeless—to improve their conditions and move out of their homeless state. However, this creaming process may actually aid Conservative opponents of aid for the homeless over time. By facilitating the departure of some of the cream of the homeless from the ranks of the collective homeless, the McKinney Act may actually facilitate the idea that homelessness can be overcome if the homeless truly want to overcome it. In effect, Conservatives may hold up individual success stories made possible by the McKinney Act's programs in support of their claims that the homeless are indeed homeless by choice.

This example highlights the tensions that exist between the more mainstream and the critical interpretations of this discourse. Clearly, there are the difficulties inherent in trying to meet these disparate goals. Very often acting to meet any one of these goals works against another goal. Therefore, we rarely get to decide between clearly right and wrong options. This means that there is no one set of fixed rules that we can rely upon to guide our actions when attempting to address homelessness—or any other social problem for that matter. This state of affairs requires that we act on a case-by-case basis. More often than not we can do no better than to choose a less offensive or less oppressive option. This requires that we carefully weigh our options before acting on behalf of the homeless. It requires that we consider not only the immediate material consequences of a policy, but also the likely long-term, rhetorical effects of a policy. And it requires that we be willing to compromise and to appear inconsistent at times.

CRITICAL SELF-APPRAISAL

Like the ideal proletarian revolutions described by Marx at the start of this chapter, critical theories should be critical of their own complicity in fostering oppression. In chapter 1, I presented four criteria that all full-fledged critical theories should meet. The last of these criteria calls for a critical self-appraisal of one's work. Accordingly, I review my efforts here in light of each of these criteria in turn. First, a critical theory should provide an explanation of how structural arrangements and social conventions foster oppression. Toward this end, my analyses in chapters 3, 4 and 5 illustrate several prominent ideographs, social constructions associated with the poor and homeless, and very general perspectives on poverty and homelessness. I use these perspectives to indicate different discourses and to indirectly point to earlier regimes of truth. These discourses, perspectives on personal and government responsibility, ideographs and social constructions serve as the foundation for economic, social and cultural arrangements that facilitate homelessness. Therefore, my work addresses the first criterion.

However, a more fully-developed critical theory would not have stopped at the point I do. A more comprehensive critical theory would provide a more detailed account of how these foundations are related to specific economic, social, and cultural arrangements. Such a critical theory would also develop a better account of how those arrangements themselves foster homelessness.

Second, a critical theory should provide an alternative vision of social relations that makes sense to and may be accepted by those experiencing oppression. Clearly, I do not adequately provide such a vision. For the most part, this work remains at an abstract level and rarely makes the bridge between critical analyses and specific conditions of homelessness.

Perhaps the closest I come to such a vision is my occasional reference to the establishment of an entrenched discourse that is not founded upon notions of merit or the clear distinction between the deserving and undeserving. However, by alluding to earlier regimes of truth and by presenting the various discourses, perspectives toward poverty and homelessness, and social constructions of the poor and homeless as historical products as flexible and even changeable, I offer support for the proposition that alternative visions are possible. Nevertheless, I do not adequately develop an alternative vision, and therefore, I fail to meet the second criterion.

Third, a critical theory should be accessible to those who are experiencing oppression—in this case, the homeless. Despite my efforts to use jargon sparingly, to explain the jargon that I do use, and to present my work in a straightforward manner, my work is far from accessible to most homeless persons. In fact, as one graduate student colleague explained, it is not very accessible to those who are unfamiliar with critical theory.

In my defense, part of the difficulty lies in the fact that I am trying to make sense of and analyze very complex structural relations and systems of thought. It is difficult to present abstract ideas in concrete ways without first backtracking and explaining everything. But to do so would distract readers from the analyses themselves and would quickly prove wearisome. Accordingly, sometimes using specialized jargon as shorthand is appropriate. Not all jargon is unnecessarily obscure. Sometimes jargon conveys a more nuanced idea than a similar, more familiar word does. Therefore, I chose to use some jargon in this project. However, because of this, non-academic readers, including many if not most homeless and even academics who are unfamiliar with critical theory, may find my work difficult to follow.

But to be honest, this work is directed at academics and privileged supporters of homeless persons, not at the homeless. While I aspired to produce a critical theory that would be useful for both the oppressed and for their academic supporters, I did not achieve this goal. Therefore, upon reflection, I fail to meet my own goal to offer a critical theory of homelessness. Instead, this effort might better be thought of as a partial or initial critical theory. However, my analyses may serve as a valuable component of an overall critical theory of homelessness.

Notes

NOTES TO CHAPTER ONE

1. Many others have employed approaches consistent with and/or as sophis-ticated as Marx's own, including contemporaries of Marx, such as Max Stirner (1995). Still, I rely upon Marx's work for explanatory purposes. I do so because of the crucial role that Marx's work has come to play in nineteenth-century, twentieth-century, and contemporary social and politi-cal philosophy (see Leonard, 1990, p. 4).

2. Although Marx did not directly address these issues, his understanding of language was more sophisticated than presented above (see Marx & Engels, 1974, p. 51). Some theorists have worked to bridge the gap between theories of ideology, theories of language, and depictions of the individual in Western discourse. For example, Liam Greenslade (1996) presents V. N. Volosinov (c. 1894–1934) as one such theorists working from a Marxist perspective.

3. There are numerous ways to approach the term "ideology." As only one example, Raymond Guess distinguishes between three research contexts lead-ing to different theoretical understandings of ideology: an "anthropological" context that emphasizes description and explanation; a "pejorative" context that focuses on critical evaluation; and an "ideology in the positive sense" context. Guess writes: "Whereas an ideology in any of the descriptive senses is something one *finds* . . . and an ideology in the pejorative sense is some-thing one finds and isolates in order to criticize, an ideology in the positive sense isn't something 'out there' to be found . . . but . . . something *to be* con-structed, created, or invented . . ." (1981, p. 23). While my use of the term is primarily "pejorative," it also draws upon understandings of ideology found in the "ideology in the positive sense" context.

4. The term "discourse" has multiple uses. For example, in the field of linguis-tics, it usually refers to the utterances, conversational patterns, speech acts, and other forms of verbal communication actually employed by a speaker. However, Mikhail Bakhtin argues that discourse also entails the social con-text in which utterances are made. For Bakhtin, "the meaning of an utter-ance includes the position of the speaker (as social subject, refracted in the other), the horizon (the meaning and values) of the listener, and the histori-cal materiality of language itself (the multiple meanings of words as they

are used in other discourses, past, present, and future, for other ends)"
(Makaryk, 1993, p. 535; cf. Foucault, 1991b). Further, Barthes argues that
cultural artifacts and practices such as movies, photographs and sporting
events communicate social discourses and thus may be read as social texts
(1972a).

5. Pauline Rosenau explains: "Critics argue that post-modernism erases the
difference between truth and error (or between theory and nonsense) and
that this opens the door to nihilism. 'Since there is no truth, there is no
error either, and all beliefs are equal' (Scholes, 1989, p. 56). Vattimo, a
skeptical post-modernist, acknowledges the validity of this complaint and
argues that nihilism is a respected and viable philosophical tradition"
(Rosenau, 1992, p. 90). Furthermore, many critics argue that postmodern
critical theorists' own epistemological and ontological assumptions undercut their ability to act. Critics often argue that postmodern critical theorists are inconsistent in offering critiques since critique implies that there is
a more correct or more highly valued standard against which the object of
critique is judged.

6. For an excellent introduction to Habermas's work, see David Ingram's
Habermas and the Dialectic of Reason (1987).

7. Some go so far as to suggest that communicative rationality as envisioned
in the ideal speech situation can lead to universally applicable principles
for creating a just society. But this goes beyond the purpose for which
Habermas introduced the concept. As Habermas explains, "We do not
need to imagine the ideal speech situation as a utopian pattern for an
emancipated society. I am using it only for the reconstruction of the concept of reason . . ." (reprinted in Horster, 1992, p. 97).

NOTES TO CHAPTER TWO

1. While many experience sensations and altered states of consciousness through
various methods (for example, through selective drug use, sexual practices, or
some forms of yoga and meditation), the very extra-linguistic nature of these
experiences prevents us from meaningfully communicating those sensations
or states of consciousness to others. We can talk about the method employed
to achieve the experience, but we have difficulty effectively talking about the
experiences themselves. In such cases, language seems to fail us.

2. One may ask, who are these ordinary people? The "rest of us" or "ordinary people" apparently are hard-working, honest, family-oriented, heterosexual and Christian, if one gives credence to political rhetoric
employed in domestic policy debate in the decades immediately before and
after the McKinney Act's passage (cf. Kyle, 2001a).

3. George Lukács, a scholar writing from within the Marxist tradition, popu-
larized the term "reification." Accordingly, reification is often associated
with Marxist analyses. Roland Barthes (1972a) employs the terms
depoliticized speech and *myth* to discuss a similar process, but without the
Marxist connotations. Depoliticized speech is an active non-description of
how the power of human relations shapes perceptions of reality. He writes:

"Myth has the task of giving an historical intention a natural justification and making contingency appear eternal" (1972a, p. 142).

4. For an excellent example of an extended ideographic analysis, see Hasian's *The Rhetoric of Eugenics in Anglo-American Thought* (1996).

NOTES TO CHAPTER THREE

1. The National Coalition for the Homeless (1999) reports that Congress appointed $712 million for McKinney Act programs during 1987 and 1988. However, that figure differs from actual expenditures as reported in an Interagency Council on Homeless figure entitled "McKinney Homeless Funding Levels," provided by George Ferguson (1997). According to that figure, actual expenditures on McKinney Act programs during 1987 and 1988 were over $756 million.

2. For an excellent, title-by-title account of the McKinney Act of 1987 and summaries of its amendments, see Maria Foscarinis's "The Federal Response: The Stewart B. McKinney Homeless Assistance Act" (1996a).

3. Information provided by George Ferguson of the ICH during a personal interview conducted at the Housing and Urban Development building on September 3, 1997.

4. The report estimated that between 192,000 and 586,000 people were homeless on a given night. The report's most reliable estimate suggested that there were between 250,000 and 350,000 homeless people on a given night. Today the number of homeless people is still contested, although Mary Ellen Hombs' and Mitch Snyder's number of 3 million continues to appear. For example, the National Law Center on Homelessness and Poverty's website claims, "Over the past year, over 3 million men, women, and children were homeless" (2005). Moreover, in its document entitled "Key Data Concerning Homeless Persons in America" (2004), the Center estimates that between 2.3 million and 3.5 million people are likely to experience homelessness in any given year. Similarly, the Urban Institute (2000) estimates that "3.5 million people, 1.35 million of them children, are likely to experience homelessness in a given year" (reported in National Coalition for the Homeless, 2002).

5. Among the polls Manrique reviewed are: a nationwide Media General/Associated Press poll of November, 1988; a New York Times/CBS News nationwide poll conducted just prior to President Bush's taking office in 1989; and a New York Times/WCBS News TV poll conducted in June, 1989.

6. Republican Congressman Stewart B. McKinney was among the Congressional members participating in the "Grate American Sleep-out." Congressman McKinney was HIV positive at the time. He contracted pneumonia during the event and died of complications before final approval of the homeless legislation. In honor of his commitment to the homeless, the legislation was named for him.

7. While such media coverage was not uncommon, many advocates did not perceive this positive bias. For example, Abraham Gerges complained: "One of

the problems has been that the press . . . always put the picture of the derelict on the bench, and that's how people think almost throughout this nation about homelessness" (reprinted in Committee on Banking, 1987, p. 104).

8. Many self-help programs, especially the seemingly ubiquitous 12-step programs inspired by Alcoholics Anonymous, apply the disease model to whatever condition or addiction they address. Many of these programs follow rigid regimes (e.g., 12 steps). They reinforce the idea that participants are powerless to completely overcome whatever particular condition or addiction with which they are inflicted. At the same time, they direct participants to take individual responsibility for their situations (for a more detailed discussion, see Peele, 1995). In doing so, participants are directed to look away from social, cultural, political, and economic factors facilitating their behavior and/or underpinning their situation. Instead they are directed to focus upon their own individual behavior. Participants are told that they are personally responsible for their fate. Furthermore, because they cannot be cured (after all, from such a perspective, alcoholism, drug abuse, spouse and child abuse, inappropriate behavior resulting from having grown up the child of an alcoholic, etc., are diseases), they must continually work on themselves. In doing so, extra-individual factors facilitating participants' life situations are likely to go unexamined.

9. There are numerous interesting points and themes in this chapter. For example, gender, ethnicity, sexuality, class, and notions of family are five other very obvious factors which greatly effect consideration of homelessness. However, as suggested in the introduction, excellent studies and critiques approaching social welfare policy and social problems such as homelessness with these concerns in mind have been conducted.

10. For an excellent review of the literature on this policy decision and its consequences, see David Mechanic's and David A. Rochefort's article, "Deinstitutionalization: An Appraisal of Reform" (1990).

11. For an in-depth discussion of such assumptions, see Quentin Skinner's 1988 work, "Some Problems in the Analysis of Political Thought and Action" (cf. Hume, 1992).

NOTES TO CHAPTER FOUR

1. I do not mean to suggest that these are the only policies that have affected/reflect these regimes of truth—and by extension, the McKinney Act—or that these particular policies developed free of the influence of earlier policies. Each of these policies developed in a particular social, political, and cultural context; contexts that included the rhetorical and legal affects of earlier policies. As William Chambliss suggests, legislative innovations usually are preceded by earlier laws that establish a climate favorable for the later innovations (1964, p. 68).

2. All quotes are reprinted exactly as they appear in the text from which they were taken.

3. Although Parliament was called in 1349 and probably would have made the ordinance a statute, Parliament did not convene due to the plague. The

ordinance was eventually affirmed as a statute during the reign of King Richard II in 1378 (2 Rich. II., stat. 1, c. 8).

4. For a more detailed discussion concerning how this approach came to prominence and became the central government's chosen method of addressing poverty, see Slack's *The English Poor Law, 1531–1782* (1995, pp. 11–13) and E. M. Leonard's *The Early History of English Poor Relief* (1900, pp. 61–66).

5. For an in-depth discussion of the impact of English laws and legal culture on the early New England colonies, see Robert W. Kelso's *The History of Public Poor Relief in Massachusetts 1620–1920* (1922; especially chapters 1 and 2).

6. Many authors and sources use the terms "alms-house," "work house," and "poor house" interchangeably. Accordingly, I use the term "alms-house" to refer to them as well.

7. Robert M. Adams writes: "It was unusual at that time for a layman to have legal training; but More, who is going to attribute cruel and stupid opinions to this man, wants to dissociate him from the Church and the Cardinal" (1975, p. 11). These "cruel and stupid opinions" are consistent with the Keeper of Order perspective.

8. Edward D. Berkowitz and Kim McQuaid (1992) argue that the business community in the United States preceded many states and the federal government in establishing and maintaining a number of social welfare-type policies in the mid nineteenth century. They suggest that these private measures influenced the development of governmental social welfare programs.

NOTES TO CHAPTER FIVE

1. Evidence bolstering Caplan's claims can be found in Alix Spiegel's report of how the American Psychiatric Association (APA) decided to remove homosexuality from the DSM as a psychiatric disorder (Spiegel, 2002). Spiegel presents a detailed account of the internal and external political maneuvers undertaken by a small number of gay psychiatrists and allies committed to change the DSM. From this account, it is clear that the APA's decision to alter the DSM in this regard was anything but "scientific."

2. This is not to belittle the good that shelter workers employing scientific studies have done on behalf of those who need assistance. The classification/designation of some homeless as mentally ill and/or as drug abusers has allowed some homeless to receive important assistance they would not otherwise have received. Nevertheless, the lack of consensus among medical and scientific professionals concerning categories of mental illness, effectiveness of treatments, etc., is reason for concern since shelter workers and social workers are influenced by, and make use of, this knowledge in their work with homeless persons.

3. Views of mental illness and drug addiction outside the United States differ significantly from U.S. views. As only one example, Annamarie Oliverio and Pat Lauderdale (1996) show that European medical professionals are far less likely to diagnose a child with Attention Deficiency Disorder than their U.S. counterparts.

4. Dryzek writes: "Objectivism is inspired by a false account of the science it idolizes. Postempiricist philosophy of science has demonstrated that a universally applicable 'logic of scientific inquiry' does not exist. Any such set of rules is destroyed in its encounter with the history of science, especially in connection with exemplary episodes in this history" (1990, p. 6).

5. Fritjof Capra writes: "Since Bacon, the goal of science has been knowledge that can be used to dominate and control nature, and today both science and technology are used predominantly for purposes that are profoundly antiecological. The terms in which Bacon advocated his new empirical method of investigation were not only passionate but often outright vicious. Nature . . . had to be 'hounded in her wanderings,' 'bound into service,' and made a 'slave.' She was to be 'put in constraint,' and the aim of the scientists was to 'torture nature's secrets from her'"(1982, p. 56).

6. Disagreeing in large part with Merton's argument, Heilbron offers an alternative version of Merton's thesis; i.e., "where science prospered in early modern times, it derived support and reinforcement from organized religion" in general (1989, p. 10).

7. For a detailed discussion of the revolution brought about by the rise of scientific method, see Hall's (1994) *The Scientific Renaissance, 1450–1630,* especially chapters III and IV.

8. Using data similar to those used by Charles Darwin, Peter Kropotkin makes a parallel move in calling for social policy. However, his "natural" laws lead to an anarchist arrangement where mutual aid, and not merciless competition, is the rule (Kropotkin, 1910).

9. The concept culture of poverty actually originated with liberal scholars in the 1960s. Oscar Lewis (1961; 1966) first used the term to describe a subset of the poor. He suggested that while all poor experienced economic deprivation, some grew up under circumstances where poverty was all that seemed possible. Accordingly, those indigent who adapted to their situation—accepted their lot, if you will—and developed coping skills that they passed on to later generations were said to live in a culture of poverty. Katz explains that initially the concept reflected a larger strand in liberalism: "The assumption that dependent people were mainly helpless and passive, unable, without the leadership of liberal intellectuals, to break the cycles of deprivation and degradation that characterized their lives" (1989:17). As such, the concept was used to argue for more far-reaching social aid programs to assist the indigent.

NOTES TO CHAPTER SIX

1. Among the other pillars supporting and/or reflected in the discourse corresponding to the Conservative stance are: competitive social relations, the family as an institution, radical individualism and the primacy of private property over other rights, and capitalism as viewed in light of Social Darwinism.

2. For a discussion of the ways that notions of a natural gendered hierarchy affect contemporary Conservative party politics in the U.S., see Rebecca Klatch's article, "Coalition and conflict among women of the New Right" (1988; cf. Lakoff 1996).

Bibliography

Adams, R. M., (Ed.). (1975). *Utopia: A new translation, backgrounds, criticism,* New York: Norton.

Adler, J. S. (1998). A historical analysis of the law of vagrancy. *Criminology, 27,* 209–229.

Adler, W. C. (1991). *Addressing homelessness: Status of programs under the Stewart B. McKinney Homeless Assistance Act and related legislation.* Washington, DC: National Governors' Association.

Adorno, T. W. (1990). *The culture industry: Selected essays on mass culture.* London: Routledge.

Adorno, T. W., & Horkheimer, M. (1972). *Dialectic of enlightenment.* New York: Herder and Herder, 1972.

Adorno, T. W., et al. (1950). *The authoritarian personality.* New York: Harper.

Amster, R. (1999). Ethnography at the margins: Vagabonds, transients, and the specter of resistance. *Humboldt Journal of Social Relations, 25,* 121–155.

———. (2003). Patterns of exclusion: Sanitizing space, criminalizing homelessness. *Social Justice, 30,* 195–221.

———. (2004). *Street people and the contested realms of space.* LFB Scholarly Publishing, LLC.

Appleton, L. M. (1995). Rethinking medicalization: Alcoholism and anomalies. In J. Best (Ed.), *Images of issues: Typifying contemporary social problems,* (pp. 59–80). New York: Aldine de Gruyter.

Arango, G. A. (1995). *A content analysis of the portrayal of homeless persons in children's books, 1980–1993.* Unpublished doctoral dissertation. Temple University, Philadelphia, PA.

Aron, L. Y., & Fitchen, J. M. (1996). Rural homelessness: A synopsis. In J. Baumohl (Ed.), *Homelessness in America* (pp. 81–85). Phoenix, AZ: The Oryx Press.

Babst, G. A. (1996, March). *Social construction theory: Theoretical foundations and application issues in policy studies.* Paper presented at the meeting of the Western Political Science Association, San Francisco, CA.

Ball, T. (Ed.). (1987). *Idioms of inquiry: Critique and renewal in political science.* New York: State University of New York Press.

Barthes, R. (1972a). *Mythologies.* New York: The Noonday Press.

———. (1972b). *Critical essays.* Evanston, IL: Northwestern University Press.

———. (1980). *Empire of signs*. New York: The Noonday Press.

Bassuk, E. L. (1985, June 11). *The feminization of homelessness: Homeless families in Boston shelters*. Speech given at Harvard Science Center, Cambridge, MA.

———. (1986). Homeless families: Single mothers and their children in Boston shelters. In E. L. Bassuk (Ed.), *The mental health needs of homeless persons* (pp. 45–53). San Francisco, CA: Jossey-Bass.

Baudrillard, J. (1983a). *In the shadow of the silent majorities*. New York: Semiotext(e).

———. (1983b). *Simulations*. New York: Semiotext(e).

Baum, A. S., & Burnes, D. W. (1993). *A nation in denial: The truth about homelessness*. Boulder, CO: Westview Press.

Beier, A. L. (1985). *Masterless men: The vagrancy problem in England 1560–1640*. London: Methuen.

Benedikt, Moriz. (1881). *Anatomical studies upon brains of criminals: A contribution to anthropology, medicine, jurisprudence, and psychology*. New York: Da Capo Press.

Bennett, T. (1987). Texts in history: The determination of readings and their texts. In D. Attridge, G. Bennington, & R. Young (Eds.), *Post-structuralism and the question of history* (pp. 63–81). Cambridge, MA: Cambridge University Press.

Berger, P. L., & Luckmann T. (1966). *The social construction of reality*. Garden City, NY: Doubleday.

Berkowitz, E. D., & McQuaid, K. (1992). *Creating the welfare state: The political economy of 20th-century reform, revised edition*. Lawrence, KS: University of Kansas Press.

Best, J. (Ed.). (1995). *Images of issues: Typifying contemporary social problems*. New York: Aldine de Gruyter.

Blakely, S. (1987, March). House approves $725 million for homeless. *Congressional Quarterly, 7*, 422–423.

Blumer, H. (1971). Social problems as collective behavior. *Social Problems, 18*, 298–306.

Bookchin, M. (1971). *Post-scarcity anarchism*. Berkeley: The Ramparts Press.

Box, R. C. (1995). Critical theory and the paradox of discourse. *American Review of Public Administration, 25*, 1–19.

Brodkin, E. Z. (1993). The making of an enemy: How welfare policies construct the poor. *Law and Social Inquiry, 18*, 647–670.

Brosch, E. (1998). No place like kome: Orlando's poor laws attempt to regulate the homeless away. *Harpers, 296*, 58–59.

Browdin, E. Z. (1997). Inside the welfare contract: Discretion and accountability in state welfare administration. *Social Service Review, 71*, 1–32.

Brunner, R. D., & Ascher, W. (1992). Science and social responsibility. *Policy Sciences, 25*, 295–331.

Bruns, R. (1980). *Knights of the road: A hobo history*. New York: Methuen.

Buck, P. O., Toro, P. A., & Ramos, M. A. (2004). Media and professional interest in homelessness over 30 years (1974-2003). *Analyses of Social Issues and Public Policy, 4*, 141–171.

Burroughs, C. (1971). A discourse delivered in the chapel of the new alms-house in Portsmouth, N.H. Dec. 15, 1834, on the occasion of its first being opened for religious services. In E. Rothman (Ed.), *The Jacksonians on the poor* (pp. 1–108). New York: Arno Press & *The New York Times*. (Original work published 1835)

Burtt, E. A. (1955). *Metaphysical foundations of modern physical science*. London, England: Routledege & Kegan Paul.

Bush & GOP screw veterans but good! (2003). *Political amazon* [On-line]. Available: http://www.politicalamazon.com/vet-links.html Downloaded 24 January 2005.

Cahn, R. D. (1924). Civilian vocational rehabilitation. *Journal of Political Economy*, XXXII, 665–689.

Caplan, J. (1989). Postmodernism, poststructuralism, and deconstruction: Notes for historians. *Central European History*, 22, 260–278.

Caplan, P. J. (1991a). How *do* they decide who is normal? The true, but bizarre process of the DSM. *Canadian Psychology. Pschologie Canadienne*, 32, 162–170.

———. (1991b). Response to the DSM wizard. *Canadian Psychology*. Pschologie Canadienne, 32, 174–175.

Capra, F. (1975). *The tao of physics: An exploration of the parallels between modern physics and eastern mysticism*. New York: Random House.

———. (1982). *The turning point: Science, society, and the rising culture*. New York: Simon and Schuster.

Carey, M. (1971). A plea for the poor, particularly females. In E. Rothman (Ed.), *The Jacksonians on the poor* (pp. 1–20). New York: Arno Press & *The New York Times*. (Original work published 1837)

Carlton, F. T. (1912). Scientific management and the wage-earner. *Journal of Political Economy*, XX, 834–845.

Chambliss, W. J. (1964). A sociological analysis of the Law of Vagrancy. *Social Problems*, 12, 67–77.

Channing, W. (1971). An address on the prevention of pauperism. In D. Rothman (Ed.), *The Jacksonians on the Poor* (pp.1–84). New York, NY: Arno Press & The New York Times. (Original work published 1822)

Chauncy, C. (1971). The *idle-poor* secluded from the bread of charity by the Christian law: A sermon preached in Boston, before the Society for Encouraging Industry and Employing the Poor. In D. Rothman (Ed.), *The charitable impulse in eighteenth century America*. New York, NY: Arno Press & *The New York Times*. (Original work published 1752)

Cisneros, H. G. (1993, December). A death on the nation's doorstep. *Washington Post National Weekly Edition*, pp. 13–19.

Clinton, W. (1996, August 22). Remarks by the President at the signing of the Personal Responsibility and Work Opportunity Reconciliation Act [On-line]. Available: *http://www.clintonfoundation.org/legacy/082296-speech-by-president-at-welfare-bill-signing.htm* Downloaded 10, January 2005.

Cohen, C. I, & Thompson, K. S. (1992). Homeless mentally ill or mentally ill homeless? *American Journal of Psychiatry*, 149, 816–821.

Combe, A. (1972). *Observations on mental derangement*. Demar, NY: Scholars' Facsimiles & Reprints, Inc. (Original work published 1834)

Committee on Banking, Finance and Urban Affairs, House of Representatives. (1987). Hearing before the Subcommittee on Housing and Community

Development of the Committee on Banking, Finance and Urban Affairs, House of Representatives, One-Hundredth Congress, first session on H.R. 558. Washington, DC: Government Printing Office.

Condit, C. M. (1990). Rhetorical criticism and audiences: The extremes of McGee and Leff. *Western Journal of Speech Communication, 54,* 330–345.

———. (1987). Democracy and civil rights: The universalizing influence of public argumentation. *Communication Monographs, 54,* 1–18.

Connell, R. W. (1992). A very straight gay: Masculinity, homosexual experience, and the dynamics of gender. *American Sociological Review, 57,* 735–751.

Conner, R. (1993). Aggressive panhandling laws: Do these statutes violate the Constitution? No: A solution to intimidation. *ABA Journal, 79,* 40–41.

Connolly, W. E. (1991). *Identity\difference.* Ithaca, NY: Cornell University Press.

Conrad, P., & Schneider, J. W. (1985). *Deviance and medicalization, from badness to sickness.* Columbus, OH: Merrill Pub. Co.

Cook, T., & Braithwaite, G. (1979). A problem for whom? In T. Cook (Ed.), *Vagrancy: Some New Perspectives* (pp. 1–10). London: Academic Press.

Council on Scientific Affairs. (1989). Health care needs of homeless and runaway youths. *Journal of the American Medical Association, 262,* 1358–1361.

Cray, Jr., R. E. (1988). *Paupers and poor relief in New York City and its rural environs, 1700–1830.* Philadelphia: Temple University Press.

Cushing, H. M., & Ruch, G. M. (1927). An investigation of character traits in delinquent girls. *The Journal of Applied Psychology,* XI, 1–7.

Darwin, C. (1896). *The descent of man and selection in relation to sex.* New York: Appleton.

Dean, M. (1990). *The constitution of poverty: Toward a genealogy of liberal governance.* New York: Routledge.

Dear, M. & Gleeson, B. (1991). Community attitudes toward the homeless. *Urban Geography, 12,* 155–176.

Dennis, D. (1996). *Under the sign of Saturn.* Unpublished doctoral dissertation, Arizona State University, Tempe, Arizona.

Derrida, J. (1974). *Of grammatology.* Baltimore, MD: Johns Hopkins University Press.

———. (1981). *Positions.* Chicago: University of Chicago Press.

———. (1994). Spectres of Marx. *New Left Review, 205,* 31–58.

Devine, E. T. (1913). *Misery and its causes.* New York: The MacMillan Company.

Di Anni, D. (Producer and Director) (1993). *The deadly deception* [Videorecording]. Available from Films for the Humanities & Sciences, P. O. Box 205, Princeton, NJ: 08543.

Donovan, M. C. (1993). Social constructions of people with AIDS: Target populations and United States policy, 1981–1990. *Policy Studies Review, 12,* 3–29.

Douglas, P. H. (1936). *Social security in the United States.* New York: Whittlesey House.

Dreyfus, H. L., & Rabinow, P. (1982). *Michel Foucault: Beyond structuralism and hermeneutics.* Chicago: The University of Chicago Press.

Dryzek, J. S. (1989). Policy sciences of democracy. *Polity, 22,* 97–118.

———. (1990). *Discursive democracy: Politics, policy, and political science.* Cambridge, MA: Cambridge University Press.

———. (1996). *Democracy in capitalist times: Ideals, limits, and strategies*. New York: Oxford University Press.

Eagleton, T. (1983). *Literary theory: An introduction*. Minneapolis, MN: University of Minnesota Press.

Ebert, T. L. (1994). Subalterity and feminism in the moment of the (post)modern: The materialist re-turn. *Alternative Orange Spring*, 1994, 22–27.

Eco, U. (1992). *Interpretation and overinterpretation*. Cambridge, MA: Cambridge University Press.

Eden, Sir. F. M. (1797). *The state of the poor: A history of the labouring classes in England, from the conquest to the present time, vol. 1.* London: J. Davis.

Feldhay, R. & Elkana, Y. (1989). Editor's introduction. *Science in Context*, 3, 1–8.

FEMA (U.S. Federal Emergency Management Agency). *Homelessness: The reported condition of street people and other disadvantaged people in cities and countries throughout the nation*. Washington, DC: Federal Emergency Management Agency Emergency Food and Shelter Program.

Fessler, P. & Elving, R. D. (1987, July). Reluctant White House approval expected: $443 million homeless aid bill cleared for Reagan's signature. *Congressional Quarterly*, 1452–1453.

Fish, S. (1989). *Doing what comes naturally*. Durham, NC: Duke University Press.

Forester, J. (1993). *Critical theory, public policy, and planning practice: Toward a critical pragmatism*. Albany, NY: SUNY Press.

Foscarinis, M. (1996a). The federal response: The Stewart B. McKinney Homeless Assistance Act. In J. Baumohl (Ed.), *Homelessness in America* (pp. 160–171). Phoenix, AZ: Oryx Press.

———. (1996b). Downward spiral: Homelessness and its criminalization. *Yale Law & Policy Review*, 14,

Foucault, M. (1965). *Madness and civilization: A history of insanity in the age of reason*. New York: Random House

———. (1978). *The history of sexuality: An introduction*. New York: Penguin Books.

———. (1979). *Discipline and punish*. New York: Vintage Books.

——— (1981). *Remarks on Marx: Conversations with Duccio Trombadori*. New York: Semiotext(e).

———. (1984a). Truth and power. In P. Rabinow (Ed.), *The Foucault reader* (pp. 52–75). New York: Pantheon Books.

———. (1984b). What is enlightenment? In P. Rabinow (Ed.), *The Foucault reader* (pp. 32–51). New York: Pantheon Books.

———. (1989). Classifications on the question of power. In *Foucault live* (pp. 179–192). New York. Semiotext(e).

———. (1991). Politics and the study of discourse. In G. Gurchell, C. Gordon, & P. Miller (Eds.), *The Foucault Effect: Studies In governmentality* (pp. 53–72). Chicago: University of Chicago Press.

Francis, A., Widiger, T. A., First, M. B., Pincus, H. A., Tilly, S. M., Miele, G. M., & Davis, W. W. DSM-IV: Toward a more empirical diagnostic system. *Canadian Psychology. Pschologie Canadienne*, 32, 171–173.

Freedman, E. (2002). *No turning back: The history of feminism and the future of women*. New York: Ballantine.

Freire, P. (1970). *Pedagogy of the oppressed.* New York: Seabury Press.

Frey, J. P. (1913). The relationship of scientific management to labor. *Journal of Political Economy,* XXI, 400–411.

Goodfellow, Marianne. (1999). Rural homeless shelters: A comparative analysis. *Journal of Social Distress and the Homeless,* 8, 21–35.

Goodfellow, M., & Parish, K. (2000). Continuum of care for the rural homeless: Examination of three cases. *Sociological Viewpoints,* 16, 32–45.

Gore, Jr., A. (1987). *Congressional Rec,* March 1987, S3683.

———. (1990). Public policy and the homeless. *American Psychologist,* 45, 960–962.

Gramsci, A. (1971). *Selections from the prison notebooks.* New York: International Publishers.

Greene, J. C. (1981). *Science, ideology, and world view: Essays in the history of evolutionary ideas.* Berkeley, CA: University of California Press.

Greenslade, L. (1996). V.N. Volosinov and social psychology: Towards a semiotic of social practice. In I. Parker & Spears, R. (Eds.), *Psychology and society: Radical theory and practice.* (pp. 116–127). London: Pluto Press.

Gregory, D. (1979). *Ideology, science and human geography.* New York: St. Martin's Press.

Guedalla, P. (1936). *The hundred years.* London: Hodder and Stoughton, Limited.

Guess, Raymond. (1981). *The idea of a critical theory: Habermas and the Frankfurt School.* New York: Cambridge University Press.

Guzicki, M., & Toro, P. A. (2002). Changes in public opinion on homelessness from 1994 to 2001. [On-line]. Available: http://sun.science.wayne.edu/~ptoro/mgapa3.pdf

Downloaded 18 January 2005.

Haas, S. (1990). *Hearing voices: Reflections of a psychology intern.* New York: Plume.

Habermas, J. (1984). *The theory of communicative action, volume 1, Reason and the rationalization of society.* Boston: Beacon Press.

———. (1987a). *The theory of communicative action, volume 2, System and lifeworld: A critique of functionalist reason.* Boston: Beacon Press.

———. (1987b). *The philosophical discourse of modernity: Twelve lectures.* Cambridge, MA: MIT Press.

Hackey, R. B., & Whitehouse, P. (1996). Managed care and medicaid: A critical appraisal. *Critical Sociology,* 22, 3–27.

Hall, M. B. (1994). *The scientific renaissance 1450–1630.* New York: Dover Publications.

Handler, J. F., & Hasenfeld, Y. (1991). *The moral construction of poverty: Welfare reform in America.* Newbury Park, CA: Sage Publications.

Harding, S. (1986). *The science question in feminism.* Ithaca and London: Cornell University Press.

Harvard Law Review. (1994). Dethroning the welfare queen: The rhetoric of reform. *Harvard Law Review,* 107, 212–230.

Hasian, Jr., M. A. (1996). *The rhetoric of eugenics in Anglo-American thought.* Athens, GA: The University of Georgia Press.

Heilbron, J. L. (1989). Science in the church. *Science in Context,* 3, 9–28.

Hicks, L. (1998). MillStoners. *New Times, 29*, 3.

Hogan, N. L. (1995). The social construction of target populations and the transformation of prison-based AIDS policy: A descriptive case study. *Journal of Homosexuality, 32*, 77–91.

hooks, bell. (1981). *Ain't I a Woman: Black women and feminism.* Boston: South End Press.

Hopper, K. (2003). *Reckoning with homelessness.* Ithica, NY: Cornell University Press.

Holloway, C. (1987). U.S. Congress. Congressional Rec. 1987 100th Cong., 1st sess., Vol.133, no. 34. H1021–2. Washington DC: U.S. Government Printing Office.

Holthouse, D. (1998). Meet the crusties: Spanging, squatting and looking for hot dog Jesus with Tempe's street kids. *New Times, 29*, 4–29.

Hombs, M. E., & Snyder, M. (1982). *Homelessness in America: A forced march to nowhere.* Washington, DC: The Community for Creative Non-violence.

Horkheimer, M. (1947). *Eclipse of reason.* New York: The Seabury Press.

Horowitz, C. F. (1989). Mitch Snyder's phony numbers: The fiction of three million homeless. *Policy Review, 49*, 66–69.

Horster, D. (1992). *Habermas: An introduction.* Philadelphia, PA: Pennbridge Books.

Howard, D. S. (1943). *The WPA and federal relief policy.* New York: Russell Sage Foundation.

Howard, J. A., & Allen, C. (Eds). (2000). *Feminisms at a millennium.* Chicago: University of Chicago Press.

HUD (U.S. Housing and Urban Development). (1984). *A report to the Secretary on the homeless and emergency shelters.* Washington, DC: U.S. Department of Housing and Urban Development.

Hume, R. D. (1992). Texts within contexts: Notes toward a historical method. *Philological Quarterly, 71*, 69–100.

Hunter, J. K., Getty, C. Kemsley, M., & Skelly, A. H. (1991). Barriers to providing health care to homeless persons: A survey of providers' perceptions. *Health Values, 15*, 3–11.

Illich, I. (1977). *Limits to medicine: Medical nemesis: The expropriation of health.* Middlesex, England: Pelican Books, Ltd.

Ingram, D. (1987). *Habermas and the dialectic of reason.* New Haven: Yale University Press.

Jay, P. (1992). Bridging the gap: The position of politics in deconstruction. *Cultural Critique, 22*, 47–74.

Johnson, G. R. (1917). Unemployment and feeble-mindedness. *The Journal of Delinquency, 2*, 59–73.

Johnson, S. (1989). *Wildfire: Igniting the shelvolution.* Albuquerque, NM: Wildfire Books.

Jones, G. (1969). *History of the law of charity 1532–1827.* Cambridge, MA: Cambridge University Press.

Kant, I. (1963). *On history.* Indianapolis, IN: Bobbs-Merrill.

Katz, M. B. (1983). *Poverty and policy in American history.* New York: Academic Press.

———. (1989). *The undeserving Poor: From the war on poverty to the war on welfare*. New York: Pantheon Books.

———. (1986). *In the shadow of the poorhouse: A social history of welfare in America*. New York: Basic Books.

Kelso, R. W. (1922). *The history of public poor relief in Massachusetts 1620–1920*. Boston: Houghton Mifflin Company.

Kinnick, K. N. (1994). *Compassion fatigue: An investigation of audience burnout toward social problems*. Unpublished doctoral dissertation. University of Georgia, Athens, GA.

Kondratas, A. (1990). Deceiving the public. In L. Orr (Ed.), *The homeless: Opposing viewpoints* (p. 36). San Diego: Greenhaven Press.

Kozol, J. (1987). Distancing the homeless. *The Yale Review*, 77, 153–167.

———. (1988). *Rachel and her children: Homeless families in America*. New York: Crown Publishers.

Kristeva, J. (1993). *Nations without nationalism*. New York: Columbia University Press.

Kuhn, T. S. (1970). *The structure of scientific revolutions, 2nd edition* (Enlarged ed.). Chicago: The University of Chicago Press.

Kyle, K. (2000). The ethical implications of mandatory computer ownership for students. *Sociological Practice: A Journal of Clinical and Applied Sociology*, 2, 265–286.

———. (2001a). The use and 'abuse' of family in policy matters. *Sociological Practice: A Journal of Clinical and Applied Sociology*, 3, 205–219.

———. (2001b). U.S. nationalism and the axis of evil: U.S. policy and rhetoric on North Korea. *Humanity & Society*, 26, 239–262.

———. (2004). Adapting Dryzek's model of discursive democracy to policy design & implementation. *Humanity & Society*, 29, 136–148.

Kyle, K., & Angelique, H. (2002). Tragedy and *catharsis* in the wake of the 911 attacks. *Journal of Community and Applied Social Psychology*, 12, 369–374.

Kyle, K., & Israel, T. (1998). The case against chemical castration for sex offenders. *Humanity & Society*, 22, 155–187.

Lakatos, I. (1978). *The methodology of scientific research programmes*. Cambridge, MA: Cambridge University Press.

Lakoff, G. (1996). *Moral politics: What conservatives know that liberals don't*. Chicago: University of Chicago Press.

Lakoff, G., & Johnson, M. (1980). *Metaphors we live by*. Chicago: University of Chicago Press.

Lakoff, R. T. (1990). *Talking power: The Politics of language in our lives*. New York: Basic Books, 1990.

Lamb, H. R., & Talbott, J. A. (1986). The homeless mentally ill: The perspective of the American Psychiatric Association. *Journal of the American Medical Association*, 256, 498–99.

Laudan, L. (1977). *Progress and its problems: Towards a theory of scientific growth*. Berkeley, CA: University of California Press, 1977.

Le Guin, U. K. (1974). *The dispossessed: An ambiguous utopia*. New York: Avon Books.

———. (1987). *Always coming home*. New York: Bantam Books.

Lehman, J., & Danziger, S. (1995). *Ending welfare as we know it: Values, economics, and politics.* Cambridge, MA: The Electronic Policy Network.

Leonard, E. M. (1900). *The early history of English poor relief.* Cambridge, MA: Cambridge University Press.

Leonard, S. T. (1990). *Critical theory in political practice.* Princeton, NJ: Princeton University Press.

Levine, I. S., & Stockdell, J. W. (1986). Mentally ill and homeless: A national problem. In B. E. Jones (Ed.), *Treating the homeless: Urban psychiatry's challenge* (pp. 1–16). Washington, DC: American Pscyhiatric Association.

Lewis, O. (1961). *La vida: A Puerto Rican family in the culture of poverty.* New York: Random House.

———. (1966). *The children of Sanchez.* New York: Random House.

Lowell, J. S. (1884). *Public relief and private charity.* New York: G. P. Putman's Sons.

Luxemburg, R. (1970). *Rosa Luxemburg speaks.* New York: Pathfinder Press.

Lyotard, J. (1984). *The postmodern condition: A report on knowledge.* Minneapolis, MN: University of Minnesota Press.

Mac Donald, H. (1994). San Francisco gets tough with the homeless. *City Journal,* 4, 30–40.

MacKay, T. (1889). *The English Poor.* London: John Murray, Albemarle Street.

Main, T. J. (1983). The homeless of New York. *Public Interest,* 72, 3–28.

Makaryk, I. R. (1993). *Encyclopedia of contemporary literary theory: Approaches, scholars, terms.* Toronto: University of Toronto Press.

Mali, J. (1989). Science, tradition, and the science of tradition. *Science in Context,* 3, 143–73.

Mandel, E. (1978). *Long waves of capitalist development: The Marxist interpretation.* New York: Cambridge University Press.

Manrique, M. A. (1994). *National survey on public sentiment toward homelessness in the United States.* Unpublished doctoral dissertation. Wayne State University, Detroit, MI.

Marcuse, P. (1988). Neutralizing homelessness. *Socialist Review,* 18, 69–96.

Marin, P. (1987). Helping and hating the homeless. *Harper's Magazine,* 274, 39–49.

Marx, K. (1973). *Grundrisse.* New York: Vintage Books.

———. (1974). *The German Ideology.* London: Lawrence & Wishart.

Marx, K., & Engels, F. (1978). *Collected works, vol 11* New York: International Publishers.

Mautner, T. (1996). *A Dictionary of Philosophy.* Cambridge, MA: Blackwell Publishers.

McClain, L. (2002). The Bush administration's plan to promote marriage, and why it takes the wrong approach. *FindLaw's Writ.* [On-line]. Available: http://writ.news.findlaw.com/commentary/20021210_mcclain.html Downloaded 20 January 2005.

McGee, M. C. (1975). In search of 'The People': A rhetorical alternative. *The Quarterly Journal of Speech,* 61, 235–249.

———. (1982). A materialist's conception of rhetoric. In R. E. McKerrow (Ed.), *Studies in honor of Douglas Ehninger* (pp. 23–48). Glenview, IL: Scott, Foresman.

———. (1980a). The 'ideograph': A link between rhetoric and ideology. *The Quarterly Journal of Speech, 66*, 1–16.

———. (1980b). The 'ideograph' as a unit of analysis in political argument. In A. J. Rhodes, and S. Newell (Eds.), *Proceedings of the Summer Conference of Argumentation* (pp. 68–87). Speech Communication Association.

McGee, M. C., & Martin, M. A. (1983). Public knowledge and ideological argumentation. *Communication Monographs, 50*, 47–65.

Mechanic, D., & Rochefort, D. A. (1990). Deinstitutionalization: An appraisal of reform. *Annual Review of Sociology, 16*, 301–327.

Merchant, C. (1980). *The Death of Nature*. New York: Harper & Row.

Merton, R. K. (1938). *Science, technology and society in seventeenth-century England*. New York: Harper and Row.

More, T. (1975). *Utopia: A new translation, backgrounds, criticism* (R. M. Adams, Trans.). New York: Norton. (Original work published 1613)

Murray, C. (1980). *Losing ground*. New York: Basic Books.

National Coalition for the Homeless. (1999). The McKinney Act? [On-line]. Available: http://nch.ari.net/mckinneyfacts.html Downloaded, 27 January 2004.

———. (2002). NCH fact sheet # 2: How many people experience homelessness? [On-line]. Available: http://www.nationalhomeless.org/numbers.html Downloaded, 4 July 2004.

National Law Center on Homelessness and Poverty. (2004). Key data concerning homeless persons in America [On-line]. Available: http://www.nlchp.org/FA_HAPIA/HomelessPersonsinAmerica.pdf Downloaded, 21 January 2005.

———. (2005). Overview [On-line]. Available: http://www.nlchp.org/FA%5FHAPIA/ Downloaded, 30 January 2005.

Nicholls, G. (1967). *A history of the English Poor Law, Vol. 1, 1854*. New York: Augustus M. Kelley Publishers.

Nietzsche, F. (1956). *The genealogy of morals*. New York: Doubleday.

Nielsen, K. (1992). On the status of critical theory. *Interchange, 23*, 265–284.

Niman, M. I. (1997). *People of the rainbow: A nomadic utopia*. Knoxville, TN: University of Tennessee Press.

Norris, C. (1982). *Deconstruction: Theory and practice*. New York: Methuen.

OED (Oxford English Dictionary) (1989). *Oxford English dictionary: Second edition*. Oxford: Clarendon Press.

Oliverio, A, & Lauderdale, P. (1996). Therapeutic states and attention deficits: Differentional cross-national diagnostics and treatments. *International Journal of Politics, Culture and Society, 10*, 355–73.

Pear, R., & Kirkpatrick, D. A. (2004, January 14). Bush plans $1.5 billion drive for promotion of marriage. *New York Times* [On-line]. Available: *http://www.nytimes.com/2004/01/14/politics/campaigns/14MARR.html?ex=1106629200&en=6ae374dc25196b26&ei=5070&hp#* Downloaded, 18 January 2005

Peele, S. (1995). *Diseasing of America: How we allowed recovery zealots and the treatment industry to convince us we are out of control*. New York: Lexington Books.

Philadelphia Board of Governors. (1971). Report of the committee appointed by the board of guardians of the poor of the city and districts of Philadelphia, to visit the cities of Baltimore, New York, Providence, Boston, and Salem. In D. Rothman, (Ed.), *The almshouse experience* (pp. 4–38). New York, NY: Arno Press & The New York Times. (Original work published in 1827)

Philadelphia Board of Guardians of the Poor. (1971). *A compilation of the poor laws of the state of Pennsylvania.* New York: Arno Press & The New York Times. (Original work published 1816)

Phol, S. (1985). Toward a sociological deconstruction of social problems: A response to Woolgar and Pawluch. *Social Problems, 32,* 228–232.

Piercy, M. (1983). *Woman on the edge of time.* New York: Fawcett Crest.

Pierson, P.(1994). *Dismantling the welfare state.* Cambridge: Cambridge University Press.

Pinter, R., & Toops, H. A. (1917). Mental tests of unemployed men: Part I. *Journal of Applied Psychology,* I, 325–341.

———. (1918). Mental tests of unemployed men: Part II. *Journal of Applied Psychology,* II, 15–25.

Piven, F. F., & Cloward, R. A. (1971). *Regulating the poor: The functions of public welfare.* New York: Vintage Books.

Pyle, H (1995). The right to suffer. In Rinkworks *Things people said: Famous people quotes* [On-line]. Available: http://rinkworks.com/said/famous.shtml Downloaded, 14 January 2005.

Quincy, J. (1971a). Remarks on some of the provisions of the laws of Massachusetts, affecting poverty, vice and crime; Being the general topics of a charge to the grand jury of the county of Suffolk, In March Term, 1822. In D. Rothman, (Ed.), *The Jacksonians on the poor* (pp. 1–28). New York, NY: Arno Press & The New York Times. (Original work published in 1822)

Quincy, J. (1971b). Report of the committee on pauper laws of this commonwealth. In D. Rothman, (Ed.), *The Almshouse Experience* (pp. 2–36). New York, NY: Arno Press & The New York Times. (Original work published in 1821)

Ripton-Turner, C. J. (1887). *A history of vagrants and vagrancy and beggars and begging.* London: Chapman and Hall.

Rivlin, L. G. (1985). A new look at the homeless. *Social Policy,* 16, 3–10.

Rochefort, D. A., & Cobb, R. W. (1993). Framing and claiming the homelessness problem. *New England Journal of Public Policy,* 1993, 49–65.

Roleff, T. L. (Ed.). (1996). The homeless: Opposing viewpoints. San Diego, CA: Greenhaven Press.

Rorty, R. (1979). *Philosophy and the mirror of nature.* Princeton, NJ: Princeton University Press.

———. (1989). *Contingency, irony, and solidarity.* Cambridge, MA: Cambridge University Press.

Rosenau, P. M. (1992). *Post-modernism and the social sciences: Insights, inroads, and intrusions.* Princeton NJ: Princeton University Press.

Rosenthal, R. (1996, August). *Visions within movement(s): Imagining homelessness and homeless people.* Paper presented at the meeting of the Society for the Study of Social Problems, August, New York, 1996.

Rovner, J. (1987, March 7). AIDS vote gauges support for tests. *Congressional Quarterly,* p. 423.

Sackton, F. (1997, December 4). Liberal programs in United States come full circle. *State Press*, p. 5.

Saussure, Ferdinand de. (1989). Nature of the linguistic sign. In D. Latimer (Ed.), *Contemporary Critical Theory* (pp. 2–16). San Diego, CA: Harcourt, Brace, Jovanovich.

Sax, B. C. (1990). On the genealogical method: Nietzsche and Foucault. *International Studies in Philosophy*, XXII, 29–141.

Schneider, A. L., & Ingram, H. (1993). Social construction of target populations: Implications for politics and policy. *American Political Science Review*, 87, 334–47.

———. (1994). Social constructions and policy design: Implications for public administration. *Research in Public Administration*, 3, 137–173.

———. (1997). *Policy design for democracy*. University of Kansas Press.

Schram, S. (1995a). *Words of welfare: The poverty of social science and the social science of poverty*. Minneapolis, MN: University of Minnesota Press.

———. (1995b). Against policy analysis: Critical reason and poststructural resistance. *Policy Sciences*, 28, 375–384.

Schrödinger, E. (1996). *Nature and the Greeks and science and humanism*. Cambridge, MA: The Press Syndicate of the University of Cambridge, 1996.

Schur, E. (1965). *Crimes without victims: Deviant behavior and public policy: Abortion, homosexuality, drug addiction*. Englewood Cliffs, NJ: Prentice-Hall.

Silverman, K. (1983). *The subject of semiotics*. New York: Oxford University Press.

Simons, J. (1995). *Foucault & the political*. London: Routledge.

Skinner, Q. (1988). Some problems in the analysis of political thought and action. In J. Tully (Ed.), *Meaning & context: Quentin Skinner and his critics* (pp. 97–118). Princeton, NJ:
Princeton University Press.

Slack, P. (1995). *The English poor law, 1531–1782*. Cambridge, MA: Cambridge University Press.

Smith, J. (1996). Arresting the homeless for sleeping in public: A paradigm for expanding the Robinson doctrine. *Columbia Journal of Law and Social Problems*, 29, 293–335.

Snow, D. A.,. Baker, S.G., Anderson, L., & Martin, M. (1986). The myth of pervasive mental illness among the homeless. *Social Problems*, 33, 407–423.

Southern Poverty Law Center. (1998). The year in hate: Active hate group count hits 474 in 1997. *Intelligence Report*, 89, 6.

———. (2003). Intelligence report: Active hate groups in 2003. [On-line]. Available: http://www.splcenter.org/intel/map/hate.jsp Downloaded, 5 July 2004.

Spar, K., & Austin, M.C. (1984). The Homeless: Overview of the problem and the federal response. Washington DC: Congressional Research Service, The Library of Congress.

Spiegel, A. (2005). 81 words. In I. Glass (Producer), *This American life: Episode 204* (Broadcast January 18, 2002). Available as .ram format audio file from http://www.thislife.org/pages/descriptions/02/204.html Downloaded, 21 January 2005.

Spector, M., & Kitsuse, J. I. (1977). *Constructing social problems.* Menlo Park, CA: Cummings.

Stirner, M. (1995). *The ego and its own.* Cambridge, MA: Cambridge University Press.

Stoesz, D., & Karger, H. J. (1992). *Reconstructing the American welfare state.* Lanham, MD: Rowman & Littlefield Publishers, Inc.

Stone, D. A. (1993). Clinical authority in the construction of citizenship. In H. Ingram, & R. Smith (Eds.), *Public policy for democracy* (pp. 45–67). Washington, DC: The Brookings Institute.

Strachey, R. (1888). Lectures on geography delivered before the university of Cambridge, I. *Proceedings of the Royal Geographical Society*, 10, 146–160.

Tashiro, C. J. (1996, August). *What is this called race? A critical examination of the use of race in health care research.* Paper presented at the meeting of the Society for the Study of Social Problems, New York, NY.

Tessler, R. C., & Dennis, D. L. (1992). Mental illness among homeless adults: A synthesis of recent NIMH-funded research. *Research in Community Mental Health*, 7, 3–53.

Thoughts and facts contributing to the history of Man. (1864). *Anthropological Review*, II, 173–191.

Tierney, B. (1959). *Medieval poor law: A sketch of canonical theory and its application in England.* Berkeley, CA: University of California Press.

Timmer, D. A. (1988). Homelessness as deviance: The ideology of the shelter. *Free Inquiry in Creative Sociology*, 16, 163–169.

Toro, P. A., & McDonell, D. M. (1992). Beliefs, attitudes, and knowledge about homelessness: A survey of the general public. *American Journal of Community Psychology*, 20, 53–80.

Trattner, W. I. (1974). *From poor law to welfare state: A history of social welfare in America.* New York: The Free Press.

Trinh, T. M. (1989). *Woman, native, other: Writing postcoloniality and feminism.* Bloomington, IN: University Press.

Tuckerman, J. (1874). *On the elevation of the poor.* Boston: Roberts Brothers.

Wallace, A. R. (1864). The origin of human races and the antiquity of man deduced from the theory of 'natural selection.' *Anthropological Review*, II, (Suppl), clvii–clxxxii.

Wallerstein, I. (1974). *The modern world-system I: Capitalist agriculture and the origins of the European world-economy in the sixteenth century.* New York: Academic Press.

———. (1980). *The modern world-system II: Mecantilism and the consolidation of the European world-economy, 1600–1750.* New York: Academic Press.

———. (1988). *The modern world-system III: The second era of great expansion of the capitalist world-economy, 1730–1840.* New York: Academic Press.

Ward, D. E. (1997). *Mothers' pensions: The institutional legacy of the modern American welfare state.* Paper presented at the meeting of the Northeastern Political Science Association, Philadelphia, PA.

Waterson, R. C. (1971). An address on pauperism. In D. Rothman, (Ed.), *The Jacksonians on the poor* (pp. 1–52). New York, NY: Arno Press & The New York Times. (Original work published in 1844)

Weber, M. (1996). *The protestant ethic & the spirit of capitalism.* Los Angeles: Roxbury Publishing Company.

Webb, S., & Webb, B. (1927). *English poor law history, Part I: The old poor law.* Hamden, CT: Archron Books.

Whang, S. (1993). *A structuralist narrative analysis of television evening news coverage of the homeless, 1985–1991.* Unpublished doctoral dissertation. The Ohio State University.

White, Jr., R. W. (1992). *Rude awakenings: What the homeless crisis tells us.* San Francisco: ISC Press.

Whitman, D. (1990). Who's who among the homeless. In L. Orr (Ed.), *The homeless: Opposing viewpoints* (pp. 34–38). San Diego, CA: Greenhaven Press, 1990.

Whittemore, H. (1990). Earnings fall short. In L. Orr (Ed.), *The homeless: Opposing viewpoints* (p. 32). San Diego, CA: Greenhaven Press.

Willey, K. (1994, April 4). School, hospitals open window into career for homeless kids. *Arizona Republic* p. A6.

Williams, J. C. (2003). *'A roof over my head:' Homeless women and the shelter industry.* Boulder, CO: University Press of Colorado.

Winter, B. (2003, June). Libertarian solutions: Solving the tenacious problem of homelessness. *LP news online: The official newspaper of the Libertarian party* [On-line]. Available: http://www.lp.org/lpnews/0306/libsolutions.html Downloaded January 21, 2005.

Wright, J. D. (1988). The worthy and unworthy homeless. *Society,* 25, 64–9.

———. (1989). Address unknown: Homelessness in contemporary America. *Society,* 26, 45–53.

Wright, J. D., & Devine, J. A. (1992). Counting the homeless: The census bureau's 'S-Night' in five U.S. cities. *Evaluation Review,* 16, 355–363.

Wright, J. D., & Lam, J. A. (1987). Homelessness and the low-income housing supply. *Social Policy,* 17, 48–53.

Yates, J. (1971). Report to the Secretary of State in 1824 on the relief and settlement of the poor. In D. Rothman (Ed.), *The Almshouse Experience* (pp. 937–1145). New York, NY: Arno Press & The New York Times. (Original work published 1824)

Yeich, S. (1994). *The politics of ending homelessness.* Lanham, MD: University Press of America.

Young, I. M. (1990a). *Justice and the politics of difference.* Princeton, NJ: Princeton University Press.

———. (1990b). The ideal of community and the politics of difference. In L. Nicholson (Ed.), *Feminism/Postmodernism* (pp. 300–323). New York: Routledge, Chapman and Hall, Inc.

Young, N. L. (1994). *There's no place like home: An analysis of the rhetoric of homelessness in a judicial opinion, an advocate's Congressional testimony, and testimonial narratives by the homeless.* Unpublished doctoral dissertation, Louisiana State University, Baton Rouge, LA.

Author Index

Subject Index